MISTRESSES OF THE WHITE HOUSE
NARRATOR'S TALE OF A PAGEANT OF FIRST LADIES

Courtesy—Frick Art Reference Library

MARTHA DANDRIDGE WASHINGTON

MISTRESSES OF THE WHITE HOUSE

Narrator's Tale of a Pageant of First Ladies

BY

IRENE HAZARD GERLINGER

Biography Index Reprint Series

BOOKS FOR LIBRARIES PRESS
FREEPORT, NEW YORK

Copyright 1948 by Irene Hazard Gerlinger

Copyright 1950 by Irene Hazard Gerlinger

Reprinted 1970 by arrangement with
Irene Hazard Gerlinger and Samuel French, Inc.

STANDARD BOOK NUMBER:
8369-8015-8

LIBRARY OF CONGRESS CATALOG CARD NUMBER:
71-117323

PRINTED IN THE UNITED STATES OF AMERICA

Dedication

This book is dedicated to all the First Ladies of the land from Martha Washington to and including Bess Truman. Each has made a distinct contribution to family and national life during her sojourn in Washington, some directly by the force of personality or talents, some by the indirect means of sustaining and inspiring husbands and children to greater endeavor. Until comparatively recent times, Mistresses of the White House had few biographers. So the material in this book was found in fragments in books and periodicals of many kinds, some of them out of print, and often in the older ones written in the highly sentimental manner of the nineteenth century. Since this information furnishes valuable source material for collectors of Americana it occurred to the writer to piece together these fragments into a stately pageant befitting the theme.

Acknowledgements

DEEP appreciation is expressed by the author to the many who contributed to the success of this book. During the years that were spent in research, patriotic reference librarians of the West Coast as well as New York and Chicago furnished a great deal of the bibliography that is included in this book. The author's debt to them is very great. Many owners loaned valued books, some of them long since out of print, which brought to light many facts about the First Ladies of the nation.

At the time that this "Pageant" was presented in Portland, Oregon with living models and authentic costumes, many friends loaned priceless heirloom garments, some of which had come down in their families for more than a hundred years. Hearty thanks are extended to all of them.

The daughter of a former Oregon Governor loaned one of her mother's lovely trousseau gowns that was brought from Baltimore years before. The daughter of an Army General represented Mrs. Taft and wore the beautiful evening gown which her mother had worn to President Taft's inaugural ball. One of the young models for an early day First Lady wore a handsome, heavy silk dress which had been made in England more than a hundred years ago and which had been handed down always to the oldest daughter in the family. So it had journeyed across the ocean and had been brought by ox team to Oregon in one of the early Westward migrations.

Copies of a manuscript relating to each of the living First Ladies were submitted to the following women: Mrs. Thomas J. Preston of Princeton, N.J. (Frances Folsom Cleveland), Mrs. Theodore Roosevelt, Mrs. Wm. Howard Taft, the second Mrs. Woodrow Wilson, Mrs. Calvin Coolidge, Mrs. Herbert Hoover, Mrs. Franklin Delano Roosevelt and later, Mrs. Harry S. Truman, with the request that they make any comments or criticism they chose and that they send a likeness of themselves to place in this book. There was a gracious response to both requests. What few corrections and changes were suggested in the manuscripts were promptly heeded. Our hearty thanks are extended to them and to Mrs. Jesse Grant, daughter-in-law of President Ulysses S. Grant and her son, Major Chapman Grant, for corrections in the manuscript relating to Mrs. U. S. Grant, and for the fine likeness of her in a gown of Civil War period which she wore when in the White House. The likeness of Letitia Christian Tyler, first wife of John Tyler, was given by Mrs. A. S. Kerron of Portland, one of her relatives; and the Harding Foundation of Marion, Ohio sent a copy of a painting of Mrs. Warren G. Harding, which appears in this book.

Acknowledgements

Hearty thanks are hereby extended for "The White House: A Bibliographical List" which was prepared by Ann Duncan Brown under the direction of Florence S. Hellman, Chief Bibliographer; and to Miss Margaret Brown of the U.S. National Museum in Washington for valuable suggestions; to Luther Evans, Librarian of Congress, for helpful suggestions as to the subject matter and arrangement of this book; and thanks also are due Mr. Henry Mills of New York, lawyer, literary critic and writer, who has made valuable suggestions.

To Mrs. J. F. Braly of Albany, Oregon, whose readings on this subject have been an inspiration to the author and to many others, my many thanks.

To Barbara Hartwell the narrator, whose own light touches and skillful cutting of the book to the length of the Narrative adds greatly to the interest of this Tale, my especial thanks.

And many thanks, too, to Chapman Grant, Major U.S.A. retired, a grandson of President Grant, and distinguished in his own right as a scientist, who wrote the Foreword.

And appreciation is expressed also to the author's daughter, Georgiana Gerlinger Stevens, a technically trained and experienced writer, who ruthlessly deleted some pet expressions, words and commas. However when she was not looking, enough words and punctuation marks were restored, it is hoped, to make the meaning clear. Children should not push their parents too far when trying to improve them!

Foreword

AMERICA today stands with a past built upon loyalty and devotion to duty of her Forefathers who wrought the hard way—the only way to develop self respect and lasting greatness—by blood, sweat and tears. They achieved the best government that the world has ever seen where individual initiative has led to personal success, the fruits of which have always been shared to further the arts and sciences for the benefit of the less fortunate.

In front of us yawns a chasm of -isms and -ologies imported from slave countries whose exponents beckon our Youth with false promises of effortless ease. In this great danger our ideals are facing it is good to read of the First Ladies of the Land, who, from every walk of life have assembled to share our National Shrines with our free-chosen leaders—their husbands.

No sermon could tell a plainer tale than the author has given us of success under a free government.

CHAPMAN GRANT, Major, U.S.A., Ret.*

* Grandson of President Ulysses S. Grant.

Contents

	PAGE
DEDICATION	v
ACKNOWLEDGEMENTS	vii
FOREWORD	xi
INTRODUCTION	xvii
PROLOGUE	1
MARTHA DANDRIDGE WASHINGTON	3
ABIGAIL SMITH ADAMS	8
MARTHA WAYLES JEFFERSON	11
MARTHA JEFFERSON RANDOLPH	13
DOLLY PAYNE MADISON	15
ELIZABETH KORTRIGHT MONROE	18
LOUISA CATHERINE ADAMS	21
RACHEL DONELSON JACKSON	24
EMILY DONELSON JACKSON	24
HANNAH VAN BUREN	29
SARAH ANGELICA VAN BUREN	29
ANNA SYMMES HARRISON	32
LETITIA CHRISTIAN TYLER	35
JULIA GARDINER TYLER	36
SARAH CHILDRESS POLK	38
MARGARET SMITH TAYLOR	41
BETTY TAYLOR DANDRIDGE	41
ABIGAIL POWERS FILLMORE	44
JANE APPLETON PIERCE	46

xiv Contents

	PAGE
HARRIET LANE JOHNSTON	48
MARY TODD LINCOLN	51
ELIZA McCARDLE JOHNSON	54
JULIA DENT GRANT	57
LUCY WEBB HAYES	61
LUCRETIA RUDOLPH GARFIELD	65
MARY ARTHUR McELROY	68
FRANCES FOLSOM CLEVELAND	70
CAROLINE SCOTT HARRISON	73
MARY HARRISON McKEE	74
MARY SCOTT LORD DIMMICK HARRISON	75
IDA SAXTON McKINLEY	78
EDITH CAROW ROOSEVELT	81
HELEN HERRON TAFT	85
ELLEN AXSON WILSON	89
EDITH BOLLING GALT WILSON	91
FLORENCE KLING HARDING	92
GRACE GOODHUE COOLIDGE	95
LOU HENRY HOOVER	97
ELEANOR ROOSEVELT ROOSEVELT	101
BESS WALLACE TRUMAN	103
EPILOGUE	106
BIBLIOGRAPHY	109
PRESIDENTS OF THE UNITED STATES	117
MISTRESSES OF THE WHITE HOUSE	119
SUGGESTED GROUPINGS FOR MODELS	121
SUGGESTED QUIZ FOR HISTORY STUDENTS	124

Illustrations

Martha Dandridge Washington	*Frontispiece*
Abigail Smith Adams	*between pages 8 and 9*
Dolly Payne Madison	" " "
Elizabeth Kortright Monroe	" " "
Louisa Catherine Adams	" " "
Rachel Donelson Jackson	*between pages 24 and 25*
Sarah Angelica Van Buren	" " "
Anna Symmes Harrison	" " "
Letitia Christian Tyler	" " "
Julia Gardiner Tyler	*between pages 40 and 41*
Sarah Childress Polk	" " "
Abigail Powers Fillmore	" " "
Jane Appleton Pierce	" " "
Mary Todd Lincoln	*between pages 56 and 57*
Eliza McCardle Johnson	" " "
Julia Dent Grant	" " "
Lucy Webb Hayes	" " "

Lucretia Rudolph Garfield	between pages 72 and 73
Frances Folsom Cleveland	" " "
Caroline Scott Harrison	" " "
Ida Saxton McKinley	" " "
Edith Carow Roosevelt	between pages 88 and 89
Helen Herron Taft	" " "
Edith Bolling Galt Wilson	" " "
Florence Kling Harding	" " "
Grace Goodhue Coolidge	between pages 96 and 97
Lou Henry Hoover	" " "
Eleanor Roosevelt Roosevelt	" " "
Bess Wallace Truman	" " "

Introduction

THIS Pageant of First Ladies has been written because of a desire on the part of the author to encourage the study of American History and thus to promote patriotic education.

As a means to this end the author had a professional dramatic reader cut the script of this book to fit a program of about an hour in length, exclusive of the time for music before and after the reading.

The Narrator read the Prologue and the curtain rose on a stage set with beautiful early colonial furniture. Seated near a small table was Martha Washington and her two small Custis grandchildren. While the script relating to her was read, spot lights were turned on the tableau of her and the children.

The next group was the other five First Ladies who belonged to the early Colonial era,—Abigail Smith Adams, Martha Jefferson Randolph, Dolly Madison, Elizabeth Kortright Monroe, Louisa Catherine Johnson Adams.

In all there were eleven groups and individuals, the individuals who held the stage alone, beside Martha Washington, being Mary Todd Lincoln and Frances Folsom Cleveland.

For each succeeding group the stage was set with appropriate furniture of that era. The last group consisted of Grace Goodhue Coolidge, Lou Henry Hoover and Eleanor Roosevelt. The curtain rose on the stage with all the First Ladies standing in chronological order. At the front of the stage beside a large United States flag, and at the end furthest from Martha Washington, stood these three last President's wives. The Epilogue was read and "America the Beautiful" was sung by everyone.

As the closing music was played, the stage lights were slowly dimmed and Martha Washington and her little grandchildren led the stately procession off the stage, with Eleanor Roosevelt the last to leave.[1]

Recordings of the Narrator's beautiful voice reading the script have been made; still pictures taken; and colored films of the stately recessional. These films, recordings, and in some cases the still pictures, will be taken into many towns in the nation where this means of visual education will be enjoyed and through which American history will be taught painlessly.

The publishers and the author hereby give permission to amateur performers to cut and fit this script to their own measure, and to amateur groups to reproduce this Pageant with their own models, old costumes, stage arrangements, etc., as they see fit. It is suggested that hats be not used, for old hats create so much laughter that the beauty of the costume and the lines are lost. For professional use permission must be

[1] At that time Mrs. Truman had not yet become a First Lady.

Introduction

granted. In the interest of giving this Pageant wide circulation among schools, churches and clubs often of limited means, the publisher and the author hereby waive all royalties to amateur performers.

Much local interest attaches to the models, who may be mostly young women with appropriate hair dressing, make-up, etc., and whose old costumes loaned by members of former White House families, or at least from the era of each President, create a stir by their beauty and quality. Some of the costumes used in the recent presentation of this Pageant in Oregon came across the plains in covered ox-drawn wagons nearly a hundred years ago.

In San Francisco a while ago a brilliant benefit ball was given called the "President's and First Ladies' Ball." Many descendants or relatives appeared from different parts of the country to represent their kinsmen in costumes handed down in their families. Two of the most attractive of these models were Elizabeth Grant Cronan and Nellie Grant Cronan of San Diego, great-granddaughters of President Grant, one of whom represented her maternal ancestor in one of Mrs. Grant's beautiful dresses.

The presentation of this Pageant by a school or other educational or patriotic group may be accompanied by a state-wide Quiz Contest, which will further stimulate reading in the field of United States and local history.

A visit to the Smithsonian Institution (United States National Museum) in Washington, D.C. to the section devoted to the statues representing each woman who has presided over the White House gives one added interest in this subject.

A small book that illustrates each of these figures and has some brief descriptive matter of the costumes worn has been privately printed by the Historical Publishing Company of Washington, D.C., and can be found in most public libraries. It is called "The Dresses of the Mistresses of the White House as shown in the United States National Museum." Its author is Rose Gouverneur Hoes, (Mrs. Samuel Laurence Gouverneur, Jr.) a descendant of Mrs. James Monroe, who was responsible for arranging this most interesting exhibit in this Museum.

MISTRESSES OF THE WHITE HOUSE
NARRATOR'S TALE OF A PAGEANT OF FIRST LADIES

Prologue

WHEN YOU visit that proud city, Washington, D.C., which has evolved in 150 years from forests, swamps, empty spaces, huts next to elegance, coon skin caps and stove pipe hats, stately mansions and back woods poverty, into its present grandeur of marble and world renowned memorials, you will see the Smithsonian Institution which contains priceless souvenirs of the growth of our country. Among its most arresting exhibits are the figures of the thirty-two women who have presided over the Executive Mansion from Martha Washington to Eleanor Roosevelt dressed in their handsomest gowns—their own when possible, in copies where necessary—the hair, coloring, accessories all as worn by these arbiters of America's social life.

It is a characteristic sequence, inspiring the imagination, for the figures represent the gamut of feminine contrasts. Ladies of the old regime dignified and aloof, pioneer's daughters, minister's daughters, school teachers, a Quakeress who was the gayest mistress the White House ever had; the strict Puritan who would allow no wine or dancing under her sway, much as Victoria would permit no smoking at Windsor, and visiting gentlemen had to lie on their backs in the privacy of the bed chamber blowing their smoke up the fireplace chimney!

There was hardship, tragedy, drama, occasionally agony in these women's lives. They battled with limited means, wretched housing, back-breaking journeys in springless coaches. They were often invalids, probably as a result of the horrible doctoring of the early periods, and often from the arduous tasks of keeping up with their husband's careers besides being mothers, often of families of eight to eleven children. They endured political slander and personal attack. Who can bear to have one's husband characterized as a baboon? Or have filthy dodgers of false scandal thrown into one's garden? But they bore it all with uniform dignity and courage, often living to a great old age—older than we, sometimes, in spite of all our sterilized living—triumphs of the spirit over the body.

GEORGE WASHINGTON
1789–1797

Martha Dandridge Washington

MARTHA WASHINGTON, born Martha Dandridge of Virginia, had on her mother's side a family of scholars and divines. On her father's side were planters and officials. They lived rather elegantly and fashionably on the Pamunsky River not far from Williamsburg in the "decorously sophisticated atmosphere of Colonial Virginia."

She was a brown-haired, hazel-eyed girl, very slim and short, quick spirited. She was very devout, played on the spinet, embroidered and knitted, danced, rode horseback, was an efficient housekeeper and a most gracious person.

At the time that George Washington met and married her, the attractive twenty-six year old Martha Dandridge Custis, aristocratic, reputed to be the richest widow in Virginia, dwelt on her own plantation in a beautiful home called "The White House," from whence later came the name of the Executive Mansion of the United States.

She had all the youthful charm, dignity and sweetness of nature which made her a favorite with every one. She had only the education afforded by a governess at home and what few books were available. What Martha Dandridge lacked in formal education, however, she more than compensated for in her inherent sense of right values and innate courtesy and kindness. Because the plantation of Colonel Custis was near her father's home there was no occasion for her to travel further afield than Williamsburg until later in her life.

Her early marriage to Colonel Custis, handsome, wealthy, aristocratic, was an extremely happy one. Three children blessed this marriage, two of whom died. Upon her son's death his widow and four children were left. So to comfort Mrs. Washington, George Washington adopted two of these grandchildren and they became a part of the family circle at Mt. Vernon.

Both President and Mrs. Washington believed in the importance of having the proper clothing and setting for their high office. It is interesting to read at Mt. Vernon letters penned by Washington after the Revolution to London merchants wherein orders were given for fine clothing and furnishings for their home. During the Revolution, however, Mrs. Washington frugally made over her clothes, and had a favorite russet dress made of raveled out silk stockings and old furniture coverings. George Washington at his inauguration wore a fine homespun suit, the handiwork of his own household. It is said by one of her family that Martha Washington always wore a white dimity dress all morning when attending to the management of her large household. The same dress was always spotless and worn for a week.

Mrs. Washington, or "Lady Washington," as she was often affectionately called, sat at state receptions while her husband moved about the seated circle of friends or stood beside her to greet those who passed by. No hand-shaking was indulged in at these stately, formal affairs, which were modeled on similar events in Paris and London. These evening receptions always closed promptly at 10 o'clock.

Reared as she had been as a descendant of the Chivalry of Virginia, who in their turn were the descendants of the English nobility, it was natural that the stately social customs of the Old World were reproduced in the first Presidential Mansion, which was at No. 3 Franklin Square, in New York City.

Because Martha Washington was essentially a home loving woman and had suffered great anxiety and loneliness on account of her husband's necessarily long absences from home because of war and public business, she unburdened herself as follows through a letter to a friend written from the Executive Mansion in New York City. Each winter during a lull in fighting during the Revolution, Mrs. Washington set out from Mt. Vernon with her carriages laden with good things for her husband and the other soldiers suffering hardships. Those winter sojourns in camp further endeared her to her husband and to every one to whom she ministered.

Mrs. Washington's letter expressing some of her fine philosophy of life follows:

"With respect to myself, I sometimes think the arrangement is not quite as it ought to have been; that I, who had much rather be at home, should occupy a place with which a great many younger and gayer women would be extremely pleased. As my grandchildren and domestic connections make up a great portion of the felicity which I looked for in this world, I shall hardly be able to find any substitute that will indemnify me for the loss of such endearing society. I do not say this because I feel dissatisfied with my present station, for everybody and everything conspire to make me as contented as possible in it; yet I have learned too much of the vanity of human affairs to expect felicity from the scenes of public life. I am still determined to be cheerful and happy in whatever situation I may be; for I have also learned from experience that the greater part of our happiness or misery depends on our dispositions and not on our circumstances. We carry the seeds of the one or the other about with us in our minds, wherever we go."

In the second year of Washington's administration, the seat of government was moved to Philadelphia. A very large house was built there for the President's residence with the hope that the Capitol would remain there and not be moved to Washington, where already preparations were under way for its occupancy as the nation's capitol. When President Washington saw the size of this mansion he declined to move into it, since at that time he would have had to furnish it wholly at his own expense. Instead he rented a house from Robert Morris and "furnished it handsomely but not gorgeously," as the chronicles say.

Mrs. Washington always returned her calls promptly on the third day, announced by a footman first. In later years White House ladies have not returned calls on the third, or any other day, by accepted custom.

Martha Washington lived through the five grand acts of the drama of American Independence. She witnessed its prelude and the final tableaux of that era. In her personal life she passed through the cycles of joy and sorrow common to many other women—a youthful, happy marriage, motherhood, bereavement through loss of two children, widowhood, remarriage, widowhood a second time—much light and joy in life, some long dark shadows, and the end of her life at seventy-one years. A noble woman whose social orbit swung in a narrow but very agreeable circle from her own White House to Williamsburg, Mt. Vernon, to New York City, Philadelphia, Washington and finally back to Mt. Vernon again. But spiritually her influence has reached down through all the years as an inspiration to all American women.

JOHN ADAMS

1797–1801

Abigail Smith Adams

ABIGAIL SMITH, a Congregational minister's daughter, began her married life with her young lawyer husband, John Adams, in a small Massachusetts farmhouse. She had had little formal schooling but she had picked up much from her father, mother and grandmother and their interesting friends, a form of education not so much in vogue now-a-days! It was not deemed advisable or necessary in those times to give women the same educational opportunities that men had. When John Adams courted Abigail Smith most of her family and their friends thought the shy country lawyer was not good enough for her.

In the early days of our country when there were few passable roads, the custom of voluminous letter writing was highly developed. Mrs. Adams was a delightful letter writer, and her published correspondence makes charming reading. With that marvelous adaptability that is the diadem of American women, wherever she went she was equal to every occasion. In

Courtesy—Mrs. Robert Homans

ABIGAIL SMITH ADAMS

Courtesy—The Penna. Academy of the Fine Arts

DOLLY PAYNE MADISON

Courtesy—Frick Art Reference Library

ELIZABETH KORTRIGHT MONROE

Courtesy—Frick Art Reference Library

LOUISA CATHERINE ADAMS

1797 she became the First Lady of the United States.

Though a Calvinist, she was tolerant and just to every one. She urged her husband to give women equal political rights. It must have taken deep affection and patience for Abigail Adams to have continued to be on good terms with John Adams throughout their lives, for he was in many respects a most selfish, tactless, and difficult person, what our great-grandparents called "a trial," which qualities caused his public defeat. Living with an Adams was enough discipline even for a Calvinist!

Mrs. Adams was the first lady to live in the White House after the Capitol was moved to Washington in 1800 and she had many housekeeping problems—difficulty in finding any one to cut the cord wood; damp plaster in the big new house; thirty servants but no call bells; doors that could not be kept closed; only six rooms completed, no place to hang out the laundry except in the East Room, etc. Though Abigail Adams had the distinction of being the first mistress of the newly built White House, on account of its many discomforts she was never very happy there and returned thankfully to her own well-ordered home in Salem at the close of her husband's term of office.

When her husband was retiring from the Presidency, she wrote, "I feel no resentment against those who are coming into power. I leave to time the unfolding of a drama."

With the passing of "Bonny Johnny," as her husband was called, the era of two aristocratic presidents ended. Mrs. Adams had suffered keenly the shock and grief that political controversies had brought to her and her husband, and they were both glad to retire to private life.

Mrs. Adams' son summed up her character in her epitaph—

"In every relation of life a pattern of filial, conjugal, maternal, and social virtue."—and yet she was a woman too!

THOMAS JEFFERSON

1801–1809

Martha Wayles Jefferson

MARTHA WAYLES JEFFERSON was the lovely wife of Thomas Jefferson, and was remarkable for her beauty, her accomplishments, and her solid merit. In person she was a little above medium height, slight and exquisitely formed. Her complexion was brilliant, and her eyes very expressive. She walked, rode and danced with admirable grace and spirit; and sang and played the spinet and harpsichord with uncommon skill. The more solid parts of her education had not been neglected, moreover, for she was also well read and intelligent, conversed agreeably, possessed excellent sense and a lively play of fancy, and had a frank, warm-hearted and somewhat impulsive disposition. She was twenty-three years old and had been a widow for four years at the time of her marriage to Thomas Jefferson. She died while her children were still very young.

Upon their mother's death, Martha, the eldest daughter, aged seven years (later Mrs. Randolph), was sent to Philadelphia to school and later was taken to Europe by her father. The two younger children were cared for by an aunt.

When Mary Jefferson reached the age of nine years, her father sent for her to join him and Martha in France. En route she stopped in London to visit Mrs. John Adams, whose husband was Minister there from the United States. Mrs. Adams' letters to friends in America describe the rare beauty, the good manners, the fine, sensitive mind of this child. Both she and her sister Martha were placed in a convent in Paris, from whence they returned with their father to the United States.

On his return home, Thomas Jefferson became a member of President Washington's Cabinet; then was elected Vice-President on the ticket with President John Adams; and in 1801 was inaugurated as President of the United States. He had been a widower eighteen years when he became President.

THOMAS JEFFERSON

1801–1809

Martha Jefferson Randolph

MARTHA JEFFERSON RANDOLPH was Jefferson's married daughter and took her mother's place as hostess in the White House. She was a brilliant woman, was well fitted to fill this position for she had been educated abroad, had enjoyed the advantages of foreign travel, and had there and in her father's home been constantly associated with men of letters and others of distinction.

She was the mother of twelve children, eleven of whom reached adult life, and many of whom she educated almost wholly herself at home, with some assistance from her father. She had the heavy responsibilities of housekeeping with large numbers of slaves to supervise and home making for her own large family, together with much care of her sister Mary's children after the latter's death. So because of all these family cares and because the journey to Washington was difficult, and Washington climate not healthful, it was not possible for her to remain long at a time as her father's hostess at the White House. One of her sons, James Madison Randolph, was the first child to be born in the White House.

Thus President Jefferson's life in the unfinished White House was a very lonely one. He did not continue the formal entertaining instituted by Mrs. Washington and Mrs. Adams, for he said so much formality and entertainment was not in keeping with the simplicity that should characterize the head of a Republic. He was really churlish about his constant playing up of simplicity. But a certain amount of social life had to be carried on, and on these necessary occasions when his daughters were not there, he summoned the vivacious wife of his Secretary of State, Dolly Madison, to be the official hostess.

During the seventeen years after President Jefferson retired to Monticello, Martha Randolph was his constant companion, an example of a charming and devoted daughter of a difficult but distinguished man.

Because practically all the old dresses belonging to the women in the Confederate States had been cut up and worn to rags during the Civil War, it was almost impossible to find any authentic garment of either Jefferson's wife or daughter to place in the National Museum's exhibit of costumes of mistresses of the White House. However, a descendant of Martha Randolph's finally produced a shawl that had been hers, and around that a costume was built. Displayed in the case with the shawl are a beaded bag, a large embroidered linen handkerchief, and a prayer book.

JAMES MADISON

1809–1817

Dolly Madison
(Dorothy Payne Madison)

DOLLY PAYNE MADISON was born in North Carolina of Virginia parents. She always attributed the beautiful texture of her skin to the fact that her mother tied a sunbonnet under her chin and placed a mask over her face to protect her complexion whenever she walked abroad!

Her family had become Quakers, but her Quaker bonnet did not conceal her sparkling eyes or her vivid personality. She married John Todd and was soon left a widow with a young son. She later met and married James Madison, bachelor of forty-three years—the kind of man who always captures the Dolly Madisons of this world!

When she became the First Lady she made many changes in the White House itself and in its social life. She engaged a competent Frenchman as Master of

Ceremonies. She changed her plain Quaker garb to gay colors, fashionable garments, and jewels.

Her philosophy of life seems to have been revealed by her oft quoted expression, "Nothing really matters enough to care deeply about it." Yet she did care deeply and tenderly for her husband. Her loyalty and devotion to him and her capacity for making friends of every one was one of the reasons for his success. Her one sorrow in life was caused by the son of her first marriage, Payne Todd, who was a scapegrace. She finally had to sell the beautiful Madison estate "Montpelier" to pay his gambling debts.

All her life she lived curiously remote from the evils of the world. True to her Quaker upbringing she was broad and tolerant toward every one.

She was direct, candid, cordial. But she was too active, too diffuse in her interests to form and maintain intimate friendships. In mature years she was a faithful adherent of the Episcopal Church, but at heart, and in spite of her gay outward plumage, she was still a Quakeress. Along with her inner calm was a joy in the rush and movement of people about her, which really was the breath of life to her. She had an amazing memory for names and faces, which contributed in no small degree to her own and her husband's social and political career.

Dolly Madison was not intellectual or brilliant or witty, but just a lively person who loved people of all kinds. She had no consuming convictions of any kind. Ease, informality, freedom, equality, together with much elegance were characteristic of her era in the White House. She was a great help and joy in every way to her husband, and she had a very good time herself. Her young niece gave this interesting testimony of her quality, "I always thought better of myself when I had been with Aunt Dolly." In that one sentence lies the secret of charm!

Upon James Madison's death, Dolly went back to Washington to live. She died at the age of eighty, still pleasure-loving, gay, a distinguished person, filled to the end with *élan vital*.

Washington people had not forgotten her gallantry and courage in helping her husband to save valuable state papers instead of their private possessions when the British soldiers burned and sacked the White House and many other public and private buildings in Washington during the war of 1812. Her bravery in saving the fine portrait of George Washington by Stuart at the risk of her safety as the Red Coats were entering the White House has never been forgotten.

I think she sounds enchanting!

A curious coincidence connected with three of the four first presidents is that they married widows; each at a previous time had been seriously interested in other ladies; neither Washington, Jefferson, nor Madison had sons; and two of them were childless.

JAMES MONROE

1817–1825

Elizabeth Kortright Monroe

BECAUSE OF HER reserved nature, and because little public mention was made of women in those days, there are only bits of information to be gathered about Elizabeth Kortright Monroe. It is recalled by her contemporaries that she had beautiful, classic features; that she framed her dark curls by a band of soft ribbon; that she was tall and gracefully formed, polished and elegant in society.

Mrs. Monroe had dignified and stately manners, and a beautiful face. She made a fine impression on the dignitaries of foreign lands where her husband's duties took them. While in France their eldest daughter Elisa was a pupil at an exclusive French school where Hortense Beauharnais, the daughter of Josephine, and the future Queen of Holland and Mother of Napoleon III, was also a pupil. Between these girls there existed a warm friendship.

When he was Minister to France, James Madison, glowing with enthusiasm for his own free land, and being a forthright and honest man, did not conceal from the old imperial regime his loyalty to the principles of representative government, which principles were being fostered by the Revolutionaries in France. This made him unpopular with those in power. Lafayette, beloved by all Americans, had been thrown into a foul prison in Austria and Madame Lafayette and her children had been cast into a Paris dungeon. Mr. and Mrs. Monroe were deeply stirred when they learned that on the next day Madame Lafayette was to be guillotined. They decided to take a desperate chance to rescue her, knowing full well that this move would cost Mr. Monroe his position. They succeeded in a manner as dramatic as the climax of a movie plot.

The next day Mrs. Monroe arrived at the prison gate in a fine carriage with all the marks of an important American official's family and asked to see Madame Lafayette. The jailers dared not offend the representative of the new American Republic and they granted her request. Madame Lafayette was released and the two most powerful men of that era, George Washington and Napoleon Bonaparte, finally effected by their cooperation the release of Lafayette from his prison.

As a result of the courage of James Monroe and his wife in befriending the Lafayettes, he was recalled from France. Prominent women of Philadelphia and Washington snubbed Mrs. Monroe because of her heroism. Probably they were the same ones who were dancing with the dashing Red Coats in Philadelphia during the bitter winter of Valley Forge when George and Martha Washington were caring for the suffering American soldiers!

When in 1817, President and Mrs. Monroe and their two daughters moved into the White House, it was said of her that "Mrs. Monroe is an elegant, accomplished woman. She possesses a charming mind and dignity of manners which peculiarly fit her for her elevated position." She received the large crowds of people who came to the occasional "drawing rooms" to which no especial invitations were issued and went through these ordeals of being a hostess at the White House with quiet patience, but certainly not with the joy of her predecessor, Dolly Madison. And quiet patience has never made a successful evening! Mrs. Monroe returned no calls and mingled with people only when necessary. Her daughters were just as aloof as she was. They could not see that the observances of official society were duties.

Because of her ill health and her temperament, Elizabeth Monroe apparently left less impress upon her time than did other Presidents' wives, but she profoundly influenced the thinking and the policies of her distinguished husband.

JOHN QUINCY ADAMS

1825–1829

Louisa Catherine Adams

MRS. JOHN QUINCY ADAMS received advantages far above those enjoyed by most American women of that day.

John Quincy Adams first met Louisa Johnson in her father's attractive house in London and they were married there in 1797. Soon after their marriage, his father, John Adams, became President of the United States and John Quincy Adams was sent to Berlin, where he and his wife played an important part in the social life of that Court. After four years spent happily there, they embarked with their oldest child for the United States—first going to Boston and then to Washington upon his election as United States Senator.

After eight years in Washington, which were the eight years of President Jefferson's administration, President Madison sent as our first accredited representative to Russia John Quincy Adams. Mrs. Adams left Boston in August with her husband and youngest child, Charles Francis Adams, leaving the two older children with their grand-parents. They arrived in St. Petersburg toward the close of October, having spent nearly three months on the journey.

Their lives were crowded with variety and adventure in foreign lands on missions for their country—London, Berlin, Paris, and St. Petersburg, from which Mrs. Adams made a long, perilous journey to Paris alone, arriving there during the famous Hundred Days. She had enough experiences to whiten a woman's hair!

Upon his return to America, John Quincy Adams was chosen Secretary of State by President Monroe. During this period of their lives, the Washington home of Mr. and Mrs. Adams was the gathering place of the brilliant diplomatic corps and the most interesting people from all over the world.

On the fourth of March, 1825, John Quincy Adams was inaugurated as President of the United States, following in the footsteps of his father, John Adams, who twenty-eight years before had been made President.

The administration of Mr. Adams was remarkable for the peace and prosperity of the country. He was the most learned man who had ever been President. The visit of the venerable Lafayette was one of the highlights of their life in the White House.

Though Mrs. Adams was more socially inclined than her husband, each of them would have been more happy with their books, their music, their quiet fireside, than with so many years of foreign residence and official life. Mrs. Adams' health did not permit her to carry on extensive entertaining when she was in the

White House, which brought much disappointment to Washington people. They were expected, as the children say, to "show off" themselves and the fine new furnishings of the White House.

Mr. Adams was (with all his fine qualities) said to have been ill-tempered and often disagreeable like his father. So life with him was often hard for Louisa. But her devotion to him remained constant. We shall never know what Louisa thought!

With the passing of Thomas Jefferson, John and Abigail Adams, James and Dolly Madison, James and Elizabeth Monroe, Louisa and John Quincy Adams, all these old friends, political rivals, colleagues,—those intimates of the Revolutionary and early Federal group —were gone. It was the end of what was called the old Ambassadorial set. New names, new faces, new manners and new customs prevailed.

ANDREW JACKSON

1829–1837

Rachel Donelson Jackson
Emily Donelson Jackson

IN 1779 Colonel John Donelson, a brave and wealthy Virginia surveyor, made the perilous journey from Fort Patrick Henry on Holston River with his family and others a distance of two thousand miles (because of no direct route) to Tennessee, and settled on land where Nashville now stands. They were four months on the journey. One of the bravest of these emigrants was nine-year old Rachel Donelson, the bright-eyed, black-haired, sprightly and pretty daughter of Colonel Donelson.

During a sojourn in Kentucky, Rachel married Lewis Robards, a man of good family but an exceedingly worthless fellow. She had grown up under difficult pioneer conditions but had developed the finest qualities of calm courage, integrity, graciousness and kindness.

Soon after her marriage her father was killed, and

Courtesy—Ladies Hermitage Association

RACHEL DONELSON JACKSON

Courtesy—Library of Congress

SARAH ANGELICA VAN BUREN

Courtesy—John Scott Harrison

ANNA SYMMES HARRISON

Courtesy—Library of Congress

LETITIA CHRISTIAN TYLER

hard times overtook her once prosperous family. Her husband had never made a home for her so they lived with his mother, who was always deeply attached to Rachel and who always took her part. Finally Lewis Robards told Rachel's mother to take her daughter back to her home in Tennessee for he was divorcing her.

At her widowed mother's home where some boarders were kept, not only for financial reasons but for the protection from Indians they afforded, Rachel met Andrew Jackson. Upon receipt of the word that Lewis Robards had divorced Rachel, she and Andrew Jackson were married.

He was a fiery, impetuous man, a brave soldier, and with all his wild turbulent nature he was a man of the deepest chivalry toward all women. No two people ever loved each other more devotedly than did Rachel Donelson and Andrew Jackson.

They had been married two years when Lewis Robards (probably out of malice) let it be known that only then had his divorce applied for years before been granted. Since there was no mail service then, no publications, or anything but occasional messages sent around by friends, it is not strange that there was this misunderstanding about the divorce. The Jacksons were immediately remarried.

After the victorious Battle of New Orleans, Jackson went there to receive the grateful plaudits of the multitude. Mrs. Jackson was very kindly shielded by the gentle women of New Orleans from making little social blunders that would have embarrassed her. Her speech and dress were homely but she had all the innate refinement and gentleness that characterizes women of good quality everywhere, and the discerning New Orleans women sensed this.

In 1828, General Jackson won the Presidency after the bitterest political fight ever staged. All his foes centered their fire on Mrs. Jackson's unhappy first marriage, the divorce that arrived too late, and even slandered his blameless mother who had been in her grave for fifty years. He managed to keep most of this evil slander from his wife. But shortly before they were to set out for his inauguration, she overheard some gossips embroidering the tale so heavily that Mrs. Jackson had a sudden collapse and died shortly afterward. The haste with which individuals and groups of people from many parts of the nation wrote eulogies about this very noble woman were mainly sincere expressions of their own feelings, but it seems that some were to salve guilty consciences and to avoid the bitter wrath which Andrew Jackson felt for those who had slandered Mrs. Jackson. The unbounded grief at her passing on the part of her slaves and servants and every one connected in any way with Mrs. Jackson were evidences of her fine quality as a woman and as a homemaker.

Since Andrew Jackson had been a poor Irish boy with no relatives of his own, he turned to his wife's family, the Donelsons of Tennessee, who were very prominent and well established people, to help him after his wife's death in all social problems. He was the second widower to enter the White House. He invited Colonel Andrew Jackson Donelson, one of his adopted sons, and Mrs. Jackson's nephew, to become his private secretary, and his wife, Emily Donelson, became his official hostess.

When this matter of what woman was to preside over the White House was decided, President Jackson asked Sarah Yorke Jackson, the beautiful and accomplished Philadelphia-born wife of Andrew Jackson, Jr., adopted son and sole heir of the large Jackson estate, to be the social head of his own large home, The Hermitage in Nashville. She often visited at the White House and she and Emily Donelson were the best of friends. Emily Donelson died in the White House during President Jackson's second term, and Sarah Yorke Jackson then took up her duties as Mistress of the White House, as well as of The Hermitage. In the last years of Andrew Jackson's life she was his constant companion and sole guardian.

Emily Donelson was a very young woman when she took up her duties as Mistress of the White House. During her regime life was unusually gay for she loved to dance and to dispense true Southern hospitality. She gave many childrens' parties, too, for her own beautiful little flock of children and their friends.

She had rare loveliness and superior intellect. Though her childhood was spent in the "back woods" she had so many advantages in meeting people of all kinds, and had so sincerely friendly a spirit that she was at ease everywhere. She had a host of suitors and married at the age of sixteen.

With all her youthful gaiety she had deep religious and moral convictions. Her firm stand against recognizing socially the wife of a favorite Cabinet officer of President Jackson's (because of serious scandal connected with her name) caused President Jackson to ask her to leave the White House. After a few months he begged her to return for he missed too greatly the congenial companionship of her and her children and the gracious skill with which she managed the White House. Not often did determined old Andrew Jackson, who had for the first time instituted in national politics the spoils system, and who was something of an autocrat, meet a force of will superior to his own.

MARTIN VAN BUREN
1837–1841

Hannah Van Buren

HANNAH VAN BUREN, wife of Martin Van Buren, was born of a fine old New York Dutch family. She possessed beauty and sweetness of spirit, together with an abiding religious faith. She and Martin Van Buren, also of Dutch descent, grew up together and attended the same village school in New York State. Her ancestors, the Hoes, had their homes for generations along the Hudson River. After ten years of happy married life, and being the mother of several children, she died. Her husband was deeply devoted to her, and gave her credit for helping him in his steady rise to fame.

Sarah Angelica Van Buren

When Martin Van Buren became President in 1837, he had been a widower for many years. His four years in the White House would have been a social failure had it not been for beautiful Sarah Angelica Van Buren, wife of President Van Buren's son.

She was a very fine and accomplished woman, daughter of an aristocratic and wealthy South Carolina family, some of whose members had fought with distinction in the Revolutionary War.

Sarah Angelica Singleton was a very young girl when she met her future husband while on a visit to Dolly Madison, her kinswoman. She had a host of admirers but chose Major Abraham Van Buren, who was private secretary to his father, President Van Buren, and who took her to the White House to live. Here she at once took up her duties as Mistress of the White House. In all of her pictures that have come down to us Angelica Van Buren is shown as holding her head very high and her hair is dressed on top of her head with three white feathers in it. Her blue velvet dress in the National Museum is probably the most popular in its entire collection.

President Van Buren brought with him to Washington many of his own beautiful possessions, among other things a set of gold spoons which he used on state occasions, but which were cited as extravagant by his political enemies and used as a means of defeating him for re-election. He was bitterly assailed also for putting some much needed alterations and repairs on the White House and for setting out trees and shrubs in the garden. But though Angelica Van Buren wore three white feathers in her hair they never symbolized cowardice and she and her father-in-law generally triumphed over stupidity and short sightedness.

Mrs. Van Buren's maternal ancestors were notable

people among whom were some leading American politicians and statesmen. She had all the advantages of belonging to an agreeable circle of intellectual and friendly people, who were always attracted by her grace and charm.

While her uncle, Mr. Stevenson, was Minister to England, she and her husband visited him in London where she met the Czar of Russia, Prince Henry of Orange, and other notables. In France they were warmly greeted by Louis Philippe and the Queen.

The life of Angelica Van Buren was an exceedingly pleasant one. Wherever she lived her home was the center of gracious hospitality. Though always having enjoyed a luxurious life, she was ever sympathetic and generous to those who were less fortunate. Her only sorrow was in the loss of two of her children in infancy. "Few earthly lives have been so unvaryingly even and free from strong contrasts," says one of the old chronicles of her day.

WILLIAM HENRY HARRISON

1841

Anna Symmes Harrison

WHEN HARRISON AND TYLER were elected to the Presidency and the Vice-presidency respectively, a great financial depression was causing much suffering. William Henry Harrison was chosen not because of a striking personality but for his military achievements in war with the Indians and because he was living in Ohio—regarded then as the Far West. He lived in a plain log cabin, which was a political asset then, just as pitching hay is today.

One month after his inauguration, President Harrison lay dead in the East Room of the White House. He had caught a severe cold on his inauguration day. During that one month, President Harrison's young widowed daughter-in-law, Mrs. Jane Findley, presided over the White House. For Mrs. Harrison had not been physically able to make the long and difficult journey from Ohio to Washington then but expected to do so when the weather was better.

Anna Symmes Harrison was born in 1776, the year

of our Independence. When on a visit to a sister in Kentucky, she met her future husband, Captain William Henry Harrison, youngest son of Benjamin Harrison of Virginia. Captain Harrison was much attracted by the gentle, modest manners and sweet face of Anna Symmes and they were married in 1795. He became the most popular General of his day, delegate to Congress from the Northwest Territory, and President of the United States.

When Indiana Territory was formed out of the old Northwest Territory, General Harrison was appointed its first Governor by President John Adams. He and his family went to Vincennes, Indiana, on the Wabash to live. Because of the many long and necessary absences from home of her husband, Mrs. Harrison for long periods at a time was left in sole charge of her ten young children on the farm. Generous hospitality was extended to all who came to their farm. She had been well grounded in religion, industry and economy by her wise grandmother.

Because no other schools were available, Mrs. Harrison had a school at her home for her own ten children and for the surrounding neighbors. There were giantesses as well as giants in those days!

On Sundays no secular matters were allowed to intrude. Every one went to church and the whole congregation returned to the Harrison home for a bountiful meal—a delightful custom! These extra guests seldom numbered less than fifty! Everything served was produced on the Harrison farm.

Mrs. Harrison did not rejoice when her husband was made President but she was trying to gather strength for the journey when the news of her husband's death reached her. In spite of the home-school, the ten children and the whole congregation for dinner, etc., she lived until her eighty-ninth year, much honored by every one. Her third child, John Scott Harrison, was the father of Benjamin Harrison, who became the twenty-third President of the United States.

JOHN TYLER

1841–1845

Letitia Christian Tyler

JOHN TYLER was the first Vice-president to succeed to the Presidency. He was a resident of what was called that "stately old vice-regal village of Williamsburg, Virginia"—(to which every American should make a pilgrimage)! It took a whole day for a messenger by horse and buggy to convey to him the news of President Harrison's death. John Tyler had graduated from William and Mary College at the age of seventeen years, and rose steadily until he became President.

He loved Letitia Christian Tyler devotedly from the first day he saw her until she died in the White House. She had an excellent mind, was a devoted Episcopalian, brought up well her family of seven children, supervised the plantation, and looked out carefully for the welfare of the negro slaves. From her letters to her children and to her sons-in-law and daughters-in-law can be gathered much evidence of her grace and beauty of person, her poise, industry and piety.

Letitia Tyler was a gracious Governor's wife when

her husband was Governor of Virginia. From her photographs there is portrayed a singularly sensitive and beautiful face. Her family were people of highest social and political influence. Her father, Robert Christian, was a friend of George Washington and a loyal Federalist. There was a large and powerful Christian family, who welcomed into their joyous circle Letitia Christian's young lawyer husband, John Tyler.

Because of Mrs. Tyler's ill health she was seldom able to take part in any of the official social life in Washington. Public evening receptions closed in those days promptly at ten o'clock at night. Occasional dances were given in the White House, "small and early" affairs, but they ended promptly at eleven o'clock. The drawing-rooms were open every evening to any one who wished to call.

Mrs. Tyler was deeply devoted to her husband, her children, her own large family, to her church and to her friends. She was deeply religious, sensitive, self-effacing, a very beautiful woman in spirit and in appearance. She died in 1842.

Julia Gardiner Tyler

1844-1845

Some time after the death of Letitia Tyler, John Tyler married lovely Julia Gardiner. When she married President John Tyler, there were only eight months before the end of his term. She was severely criticized by her husband's opponents for the style in which she entertained and the handsome clothes she wore, and because she had the names of her guests announced as they entered—which was too wickedly European for free Americans to swallow!

In spite of all the prudence and good management of Julia Gardiner Tyler, in her later widowhood she was obliged to seek a pension from Congress, which was granted. She retired to Georgetown to live in her favorite Catholic parish.

JAMES KNOX POLK

1845–1849

Sarah Childress Polk

PRESIDENT JAMES KNOX POLK was the son of a pioneer family which crossed the Alleghenies from North Carolina to Tennessee. He was a sickly boy of eleven years when this journey was made. Because he was never strong, his family gave him the best education they could provide. He went to a Boy's Academy, then to the State University at Chapel Hill, North Carolina, then studied law, went for many terms to Congress from Tennessee, was Speaker of the House, became Governor of Tennessee, and President of the United States.

Near the Polk home lived on her father's farm lovely, dark-skinned, dark-eyed Sarah Childress. Girls of that day were not supposed to have much education but Sarah's father most originally gave her and her sister every advantage. He engaged for them as a tutor one of the teachers at the Murfreesboro Academy attended by James Polk, then sent them to the Moravian Institute at Salem, North Carolina. There Sarah attained both discipline and culture.

At the age of nineteen, she married James K. Polk, who was then a member of the Tennessee Legislature, accompanied him to Washington during his many years as a Congressman, and was a very popular member of official Washington society. She had an unusually clear understanding of affairs of state and had an education superior to many of the men in public life of that day. But because women were not then popularly supposed to have brains enough to understand business or politics, Mrs. Polk wisely kept her opinions to herself and let the men do all the talking. Because she was a good listener to their often inane conversation, they regarded her as a most agreeable woman, and Mrs. Polk's technique has still to be improved upon.

Sarah Childress Polk was a deeply religious woman, a stern Presbyterian. It was said of her that she learned from her high-principled parents what may be called the "aristocracy of virtue." She held weekly receptions at the White House and she received her guests seated in a chair, as Martha Washington had done. President Adams had dispensed cake and wine to his guests and President Jackson had served cheese. But the throng which attended the receptions of the Polks became so great that Mrs. Polk omitted all refreshments at these affairs. She did not permit wine at any time to be served in the White House.

A few days before the close of his administration, a splendid dinner party was given by the President to

General Zachary Taylor who was to be his successor. At the big reception that followed the dinner that night, great throngs came to bid an affectionate farewell to this popular President and his wife in spite of no wine or cheese!

Shortly after his retirement from the Presidency, James Polk died in the very beautiful home he had purchased in Nashville, Tennessee, since then always called "Polk Place." For nearly forty years after her husband's death, Mrs. Polk mourned his passing. She received countless visitors who came from great distances and from near by to pay their respects to her, but she returned no calls and lived in seclusion to the end of her days. She had never had any financial worries or other serious problems of any kind. The one great tragedy of her life was the loss of her husband. From her early education she was given the priceless privilege of being able to enjoy her own mind.

Courtesy—Frick Art Reference Library

JULIA GARDINER TYLER

Courtesy—Library of Congress
SARAH CHILDRESS POLK

Courtesy—Library of Congress

ABIGAIL POWERS FILLMORE

Courtesy—Library of Congress

JANE APPLETON PIERCE

ZACHARY TAYLOR

1849–1850

Margaret Smith Taylor
Betty Taylor Dandridge

ZACHARY TAYLOR is another President who was born in Virginia. In early childhood he was taken to Kentucky. He came of a good English family whose connections were of the blue blood of the South. His father had served in Washington's army.

Zachary Taylor went to a small school where all the boys carried guns and stacked them near at hand. For Indians were a constant menace and some of his schoolmates had been scalped when returning home from school!

He met his future wife, Margaret Smith, when she was fourteen. He and a friend were received as strangers in need of a night's lodging by Margaret's father when Zachary Taylor was passing through Maryland to Washington on horseback. He had been hurt and Margaret bathed and bound his injured foot.

Six years later, after he had graduated from West Point, he returned to marry her.

When their children came she sent them to her relatives or to her husband's family home so that they might have the safety and the educational advantages of the settlements. Wherever her husband went, and in spite of all the dangers, she always followed him. For twenty-four years she followed him from camp to camp and post to post. He steadily advanced in military rank. One of their daughters at the age of fifteen ran away and married Jefferson Davis who was just out of West Point. Colonel Taylor never forgave his daughter—and she died shortly afterward. But in the heat of battle years later when the real gallantry of Jefferson Davis was manifested the father forgave his son-in-law.

Zachary Taylor's valor in the Mexican war brought him the Presidency in 1849 which he had not sought nor particularly desired. His wife was bitterly opposed to his acceptance of this high office for she knew he was not fitted for this position, and she longed to be settled with him in their own home after their many years of wandering. She announced that she would never personally preside at the White House. So shortly after his inauguration, Mrs. Taylor turned over her official duties to her twenty-two year old daughter Betty, who was always affectionately referred to as "Miss Betty."

With the coming of attractive young Betty Taylor to the White House, there were gradually more parties given and the social popularity of her father increased. She had sincere friendliness, social ease and tact. A wit said of her that she possessed the "artlessness of a rustic and the grace of a duchess."

After sixteen months of service as President, Zachary Taylor died suddenly. Mrs. Taylor was inconsolable and she died two years later.

While hostess at the White House, Betty Taylor was married to Major William Bliss, who was serving as Adjutant General to the President. He died in 1853 and several years later Betty Taylor Bliss married Philip Dandrige of Winchester, Virginia.

"Miss Betty" left no descendants, but she had throngs of friends and admirers. She lived to an advanced age and died in Winchester. To the very end of her life her home was the "Salon of the Valley of the Shenandoah."

MILLARD FILLMORE

1850–1853

Abigail Powers Fillmore

ABIGAIL POWERS FILLMORE was the daughter of a Baptist Minister of Saratoga County, New York, who died when Abigail was an infant. Because of limited means, her widowed mother moved with relatives and friends to a frontier settlement in Cayuga County, where Mrs. Fillmore kept boarders and Abigail taught school,—the only two occupations open to women of their station.

One of Abigail Powers' students was Millard Fillmore, two years her junior, whom she instructed and inspired to the end that he might follow a more congenial occupation than that of weaving to which his father had apprenticed him, and for which he received very little pay.

With what little education he possessed, he taught school in seasons when he did not have to follow his trade, studied law, and finally through the good offices of a friend, the balance of his time as an apprentice was paid for, and he was thus free to practice law. He went

Mistresses of the White House

on to serve three terms in the State Legislature of New York State, to go to Congress for two terms, to be elected Vice-president, and finally, upon the death of President Taylor, to become President of the United States.

Mrs. Fillmore was the most intellectual First Lady who up to that time had occupied the White House. She had always been a student and had read widely. When she came to Washington to live and found no library in the White House, she asked her husband to secure a Congressional appropriation for books, which he did.

In appearance Mrs. Fillmore was tall and fair with a fine blending of beauty and strength. The letters that passed between her and Millard Fillmore for three years when he was only a hundred and fifty miles away from her but did not have the time or the money to return to see her, attest both strength of character and delicacy of feeling, which were also reflected in his very formal letters to her. It is said that it was only a short time before their marriage that he felt he could kiss her hand lightly in parting. There was always the deepest affection between them, and her death was a terrible blow to her husband and to every one who knew her. She died only three weeks after leaving the White House following President Pierce's inauguration.

FRANKLIN PIERCE

1853–1857

Jane Appleton Pierce

FRANKLIN PIERCE of Revolutionary ancestry was the son of General Benjamin Pierce, who was the most public spirited man of his community, a man of the people and a great leader. Franklin Pierce was brought under the sway of this intensely patriotic father and a deeply religious mother. He was given a good education at academies and near-by New Hampshire schools, then went to Bowdoin College in Maine. He was a fellow student with Hawthorne and Longfellow.

While at college he fell in love with, and later married, the daughter of the President of Bowdoin College, Jane Appleton. She was a shy, sensitive, beautiful young woman who had come up in an atmosphere of culture and piety.

Meantime Franklin Pierce went to the State Legislature, to Congress, to the Senate, then served brilliantly in the Mexican War as a private, then as Colonel and as General. In 1852 he was elected by the Democrats to the Presidency of the United States.

The three sons born to them died, the last one shortly before his father's inauguration as President. In frail health and stunned with grief, this naturally shy woman braced herself for the public appearances necessary in the White House. At these affairs she presided with grace and quiet dignity, but without enthusiasm.

President Pierce was a gentleman and his term although important politically was dull socially. His marriage was an exceedingly harmonious one, however. Mrs. Pierce died shortly after his retirement from the presidency and he lived out the rest of his life alone, much beloved for his geniality, generosity and kindliness.

JAMES BUCHANAN

1857–1861

Harriet Lane Johnston

JAMES BUCHANAN was the first and only President to enter and leave the White House unmarried. He was born in Pennsylvania, made good use of his education, became a lawyer, and was engaged to a wealthy and beautiful young woman. However a lover's quarrel over some trifle parted them. She died under rather mysterious circumstances and it is said he never loved again.

His orphaned niece, Harriet Lane, became his ward and grew into an accomplished woman of the world. She was well provided for financially and had many family connections, but at the age of nine years she chose among many proffered homes that of her bachelor uncle James Buchanan.

She was blessed with abounding health, high spirits, a frank truthful nature, and a warm heart. She was proficient in music and other accomplishments. She finally decided to become an Episcopalian, though her cherished Uncle James was a Presbyterian, and she had developed a deep respect and liking for the Roman

Catholic Church during her convent days. She was a blonde with deep violet eyes that had a strange dark line around them, her face was an animated one on which her vitality and changing emotions were clearly reflected. She had perfect taste in her dress as is evidenced by the popularity of her white taffeta wedding gown in the National Museum. In every sense she was a lady.

Harriet Lane presided with quiet dignity and pleasure over stately "Wheatland," James Buchanan's Pennsylvania home; over the American Embassy in London when he was Ambassador to the Court of St. James, and where she was a great favorite at Court; and over the White House.

During their stay in the White House the outstanding social event was the visit of the young Prince of Wales and his entourage. This was the first time that English Royalty had visited the President of the United States.

Queen Victoria wrote President Buchanan a most cordial letter of thanks for the kindness shown her young son, and she sent gifts to him and to Miss Lane. The Prince of Wales had been much attracted to this charming young woman and had enjoyed the entertainments arranged for him. Some of the young people had suggested a brilliant ball, but the President rejected the idea because he said the White House was not his private home, but the property of the nation, and that dancing was strongly disapproved of by many of his supporters!

There were many great days of happiness in Harriet Lane's life. One of them was when she was presented at Court in England, and where she was greatly admired for her unaffected modesty, dignity and beauty; the day when she witnessed James Buchanan and Alfred Tennyson receive honorary degrees of Doctor of Civil Laws at the University of Oxford; and the day of her wedding at "Wheatland" to Henry Elliot Johnston. There were other events that brought her great sorrow; the death of a beloved sister and a brother and the death of her two sons in their teens. In memory of the latter she left her fortune, which was of considerable size, to a school for choir boys in connection with the National Cathedral in Washington.

Perhaps at no time in Harriet Lane's life did she show greater wisdom and skill than during the last troubled years of her uncle's administration when the Secession movement was started by South Carolina; when the apathy of Congress; the apparent indifference of Northern people; and the general pre-war hysteria of the times made President Buchanan's position very difficult. Much of all this unrest was reflected in the social life of the day and to Harriet Lane's good taste and good judgment her Uncle attributed the peaceful close of his term. Harriet Lane left the White House with almost as many friends and as great popularity as the inimitable Dolly Madison had enjoyed.

ABRAHAM LINCOLN

1861–1865

Mary Todd Lincoln

ABRAHAM LINCOLN was the first President born outside of the thirteen original states. His father was said to have been a shiftless, wandering laborer. His mother was a fine woman who died when he was very young; but he was fortunate in having a step-mother who was a vigorous woman and who gave him all the help she could. His early struggles for an education and his steady rise to fame are too well known to every one to repeat here. They are one of the chief glories of our country.

Abraham Lincoln had several attachments for beautiful, better educated and better placed women than himself. Anne Rutledge was the great love of his life.

It is said that at the time Mary Todd met Abraham Lincoln, she was engaged to Stephen A. Douglas, but that at once when she met Lincoln she seemed to know intuitively that he was destined for high office. She belonged to one of the oldest and most influential pioneer families of Kentucky. And it was of them that Lincoln, with his inimitable drawl, said, "The Todds are pretty fine people! They spell their name with two d's while God only has one." So from a flock of suitors she selected the one she felt would take her furthest, though her friends felt she had picked the least promising one. Her uncanny foresight was rewarded, however, by fulfillment of her wish; but her life in the White House had many shadows.

Criticism haunted her every move. Her Southern family were not in political accord with the President; because she liked pretty clothes and had a light, merry heart she was accused of wastefulness and levity; when she abolished state dinners and refreshments at their evening receptions as a matter of war-time economy, she was accused of parsimony.

Mrs. Lincoln's merry nature, her ambition and her complete faith in her husband's capacity to rise to the greatest heights were an inspiration to him throughout their lives together. Four sons were born to them.

From Mrs. Lincoln's colored maid and dressmaker who was constantly on duty in the White House comes testimony of the fine quality of Mrs. Lincoln as an individual and as a home-maker.

From the writings of Colonel W. H. Crooks, who was made a personal body-guard of Lincoln, and who admired him deeply, we gather much interesting information. He gives an account of the first evening reception given in the White House by the Lincolns when throngs came, many of them in full evening dress and many plainly dressed from the country districts and backwoods, some of the men having their trousers tucked into their high cow-hide boots, trampling the carpets, shaking the chandeliers and sometimes, alas, spitting tobacco juice!

Colonel Crooks also testifies that dignity, courtesy, quietness and simplicity marked the home life of the Lincolns. Their common sorrow over the loss of their son, and their deep devotion to their remaining sons were their strongest ties. Mrs. Lincoln looked well to the ways of her husband. She was much better educated, had much more social back-ground than her husband, but on the other hand was more tactless than he was and had not the saving grace of his sense of humor or his sensitiveness, or his keen insight.

It was probably Mrs. Lincoln whose influence prevented her husband from becoming Governor of Oregon in 1849, because she did not want her husband's chances for political advancement (which she always visioned) to be cut off, and because she did not want to go off to distant woods to live, "in swamps and malaria," as was said of Oregon in those days.

In any study of Mary Todd Lincoln it must be remembered that Lincoln's own nature was complex—and that her life was not easy.

ANDREW JOHNSON

1865-1869

Eliza McCardle Johnson

ANDREW JOHNSON was the only president who described himself as a handicraftsman. His father died when he was five years old and at the age of ten years he was apprenticed to a tailor. He learned to read a little from a kindly man who read to the young apprentices as they bent over their tasks through the long hard days.

At the age of nineteen years, Andrew Johnson married seventeen-year-old Eliza McCardle, a charming and beautiful Southern girl, daughter of a Scotch shoemaker and merchant. She taught him to read with some facility as he worked at his tailor's trade at night when their children were at rest and her house work was finished. And she taught him to write, though he did not learn to use a pen easily until he was a Representative in Congress. In all his youth he did not have one day of regular school-room instruction.

Andrew Johnson was greatly blessed in having a mother of noble quality; a thrifty, industrious, loyal wife like Eliza McCardle; and a mother-in-law who was devoted to him. He was blessed, too, in having an indomitable will, and he never let difficulties down him.

When Tennessee seceded from the Union, he stood fast by the Union though he was a Southern Democrat. He was the only member of Congress from the South who had opposed the secession of the Southern states. So he was elected Vice-president when Lincoln ran successfully for the Presidency the second time. Six months after his second inauguration Lincoln was assassinated and Andrew Johnson became President.

No one ever lived in the White House in more trying times than did Eliza Johnson. The whole nation was rent by the Civil War; the tragic death of Abraham Lincoln; the revelation of the plot to kill at the same time Andrew Johnson and William Henry Seward; all were hard on a woman who was an invalid.

Though most of her days were spent quietly in her own apartments in the White House surrounded by her family and her books, (for she had a decided literary bent), she was a woman of such strong character, faith and force, with sweetness, that the whole family revolved around her. She was the most influential member of her family. It is said that Mrs. Johnson only attended one White House party and that was one given for her grand-children and their young friends. No White House family up to that time had ever had a livelier, happier lot of children in the White House. She gladly left to her daughter, Mrs. Patterson, the management of the Executive Mansion.

Martha Johnson Patterson was one of the best housekeepers the White House ever had. Congress made an appropriation of $30,000 for furnishings, which expenditures she superintended. She was especially proud of her dairy. Her cows grazed on what is now the White House lawn, and her dairy was the "show place" of that day.

The White House was a wreck when the Johnson family arrived. Soldiers had wandered unchallenged through the entire suite of parlors; the furnishings of the rooms were dirty and broken; guards had spat and slept with their boots upon the sofas and carpets until they were ruined; and the great crowds that had surged through this historic mansion in Lincoln's day and in preceding administrations had literally worn out the fine old furniture and carpets.

Mrs. Patterson, who had great nervous energy and force like her father, and who had his strong will, set herself to the task of restoring through complete renovation, repairing, and furnishing this large place with the meager funds allowed. And she did it so well that every one said the President's house had never before been so simply and yet so beautifully appointed.

Mrs. Patterson presided with elegance, ease and great tact during the deeply troubled era of her father's presidency. It is said that she once remarked, "We are just plain people from the mountains of Tennessee, placed in this position by a great tragedy, and we have no desire to put on airs."

Courtesy—National Archives, Washington

MARY TODD LINCOLN

Courtesy—Library of Congress

ELIZA McCARDLE JOHNSON

Courtesy—Library of Congress

JULIA DENT GRANT

Courtesy—Library of Congress

LUCY WEBB HAYES

ULYSSES S. GRANT

1869–1877

Julia Dent Grant

ULYSSES S. GRANT was educated in the schools of Mount Pleasant, Ohio, and later received an appointment to West Point. Upon his graduation he went to St. Louis where he met and married Julia Dent, the young sister of one of his West Point classmates.

She was a slender, vivacious girl, very spirited and with great depth of character. Through all their lives together she always loved him and had supreme confidence in his ability to succeed. She followed him where possible to army posts; then through years of hard struggles after he resigned from the army and ventured into business with only failure, she and her mother always helped to the utmost. And she stood by confidently when he volunteered for army service at the beginning of the Civil War, and climbed to command of all the Union forces, through his gallantry and skill at Fort Donaldson, Vicksburg, and the campaigns of Tennessee and Virginia. He became the most popular general in the nation; then came the Presidency. "For better for worse, for richer for poorer," had not been spoken idly by Julia Dent the day she married Ulysses Grant.

Among many noble qualities in Ulysses Grant was his magnanimous nature. When General Robert E. Lee surrendered to General Grant, the latter promptly handed back his sword to him, and refused to take as trophies of war the army horses with the words, "You will need them on the farms."

President Grant believed in the principles of the newly formed Republican party and had fought to preserve the Union. But he wisely consulted leaders of both parties about matters of policies and appointments. He gradually learned to have patience with people and procedures outside the army; and he became the most popular man in the nation.

Mrs. Grant came to the White House with a fine family and social background. Her simplicity and cordiality were valuable in the reconstruction period as an asset to her husband.

President Grant was one of the youngest men to become a President of the United States and that accounted for the youth of his three sons and one daughter when they came to the White House. Mrs. Grant was always a close comrade and consultant of her husband. She once remarked jokingly, "Having learned a lesson from her predecessor, Penelope, she accompanied her Ulysses on his wanderings."

President Grant had the faculty of keeping his home life and his official life separated. He and his wife were already popular with Washington society when he became President and they and their children were an extremely happy, united family. They entertained with elegance but in unaffected sincerity and good will to people of all walks of life when in the White House. The respect of the whole nation for the Grant family carries through today to the third and fourth generations, who are maintaining the same high traditions of this outstanding American family.

The great social event of the Grant regime was the wedding in the White House of their only daughter, Nellie, and Algernon Sartoris, an Englishman—one of the happiest of international romances.

At the close of his second term, President and Mrs. Grant toured the world for about two years and received honors only paid to reigning rulers wherever they went. Thousands of enthusiastic friends saw them off at New York, and Californians turned out in great masses in San Francisco to greet them upon their return.

After the Presidency, Ulysses Grant went into business without success; a terrible crash came through no fault of his; his suffering from an incurable disease; his gallant determination to finish his "Memoirs" so that all business debts would be paid and no stain ever rest on the Grant name; his further anxiety to leave his family in comfortable circumstances; all furnish one of the dramas of American life.

Because of his superior ability and the loyalty of his wife and children, he triumphed over all difficulties and accomplished his worthy ends; so his life closed in peace. His "Memoirs" had the greatest sale of any books of their kind up to that time and are now the outstanding reference work on the Civil War. Because of the modesty of the author, their pure literary quality, and their truthfulness in every statement, the volumes have taken a permanent place in American literature.

RUTHERFORD B. HAYES

1877–1881

Lucy Webb Hayes

RUTHERFORD B. HAYES was born in Ohio, his family having come out from Vermont, people of Scotch descent, whose occupation had been that of innkeepers, blacksmiths, etc. His mother was of a fine Huguenot family. He married Lucy Webb, the first President's wife to have a college degree.

Lucy Webb was a lovely and intelligent young woman who had been well educated in the Wesleyan Women's College of Cincinnati. She had a strong and positive character and her influence in Washington and over the nation was far-reaching. Lucy Hayes represented what was called the "New Woman" era. She was the first of the White House women of the third period. The women of the Revolutionary period of American history exhibited exceptionally strong traits of character, which were perhaps developed out of the stress of the times. With the end of the administration of John Quincy Adams a new generation of men and women came into prominence. Life began to be easier for most people. The women in many cases developed into social queens, but were not expected to be anything else. They were fine women who did their home-making well but in some cases had no inclination to do anything in a public way.

Mrs. Hayes was the product of the last half of the nineteenth century, when women were slowly emerging from obscurity and asserting their right to educational and other advantages on an equal footing with men. She had in her youth come under the strict discipline of the Methodist Church and this was a powerful factor in shaping her character. She had come from Ohio where the woman's crusade against intemperance began, so it was natural that during her reign in the White House wine was not served. With Mrs. Hayes' ideas as to her own rights as an individual to determine her own course in matters social and domestic, her husband was fully in accord. Her gentle self-assertion gave other women of the nation and their husbands new light on the subject of equal rights for women.

At the outbreak of the Civil War, Rutherford Hayes entered the Army; was wounded many times; served with distinction throughout the war; and was elected to Congress before peace was declared. Mrs. Hayes had spent two years in camp ministering to the needs of her husband's soldiers and was greatly loved by them. Mr. Hayes left the army as a Brigadier-General, and at once took his seat in Congress, where he served for several terms. Then he was elected Governor of Ohio, and while in that position he and his wife extended liberal and gracious hospitality to a very wide circle of people. His wife was instrumental in bringing about many measures for social betterment in Ohio.

Mrs. Hayes not only met all her public obligations with quiet success but she was the mother of eight children only five of whom—four boys and one girl—were alive when the Hayes family were in the White House, and her home was a very happy one. She had superb health and joy in life. I can't help being glad to strike that note at last! When some one asked her if she did not tire of seeing so many people she said, "Oh, no, I never get tired of having a good time." She was of medium height, squarely built and had large features. She had a pleasing, animated face and dressed simply but in the best taste.

She delighted in giving pleasure to children and young people. No White House children ever had more good times than did the Hayes children. One of their lively sixteen-year old guests on the occasion of a White House party returned to her home in Cincinnati declaring that she would never be satisfied with any one less than a man destined to be President of the United States. She was Helen Herron, the future wife of William Howard Taft.

In addition to the many formal state receptions, dinners, etc., (which were always given with the greatest attention to detail and with elegance,) Mrs. Hayes was at home informally each evening when state affairs were not on from eight to ten o'clock for any one who chose to call. There was scarcely an evening in the week when the green parlor was not full of people of all walks of life.

During the four years the Hayes family dwelt in the White House, there was more cheer and entertaining than had occurred there during any other previous President's term. Their outstanding social event was the celebration of their silver wedding anniversary. When they retired to private life, they returned to a beautiful estate inherited from Mr. Hayes' uncle in Fremont, Ohio, carrying with them the good will of the nation.

JAMES A. GARFIELD

1881

Lucretia Rudolph Garfield

JAMES A. GARFIELD was the last president to be born in a log cabin. He had the best blood of New England families in his veins. His grandfather Garfield had died leaving his wife and several small children in very straightened circumstances. So they journeyed to Ohio from Worcester, New York, to seek greater opportunity. There grandson James met and married Eliza Ballou.

Eliza Ballou Garfield was descended from a good Huguenot family which had fled from France to America at the time of the Edict of Nantes. For ten generations the men of her family had been eloquent preachers. With this combination of New England Puritan and Huguenot ancestry, it was natural that her son, James Garfield, should be of a religious mind. He also had a strong love of learning, a capacity for thought, an eloquent tongue, and tireless energy.

All of his family sacrificed everything to give James Garfield a good education. At Hiram College he met

Lucretia Rudolph, a quiet, studious girl, very refined, of a poor but ambitious and industrious family. Later, after she had entered Hiram College, he taught her Latin. Evidently he was a good teacher and she a good student, for twenty years later she prepared their sons in Latin for college!

James Garfield preached in the Campbellite Church; became president of Hiram College; made political speeches; became a lawyer; went to the Legislature; became an army officer in the Civil War; went to Congress; and was elected President of the United States.

Lucretia Rudolph Garfield, daughter of an Ohio farmer, was one of very few women who enjoyed the advantages of a truly higher education in those days. Her love affair with Garfield was one of countless college romances that have developed and are still developing into happy marriages because of a common basis of friendship, interests and tastes.

The sojourn of the Garfields in the White House was only of a few months' duration. During her stay there Mrs. Garfield though in frail health held many pleasant White House receptions and made a very good impression upon every one. Both she and her husband had risen from humble stations in life, both had studied and worked hard, each were tenderly devoted to the other and to their five fine children.

In the days of her great trial as she watched her husband slowly dying from the shot of the crazed Guiteau she further merited sympathy because of her self-control and thoughtfulness for every one else, especially for the eighty-year old mother of the President, Mrs. Eliza Ballou Garfield, who was the first President's mother to dwell with her son in the White House. The honor that both the President and his wife showed to this noble woman set an example and reflected credit upon the First Family of the land.

If some fine characteristics shone out above others in Lucretia Garfield it was her fairness, her distaste for sham, her self restraint. Because of these qualities in her and their respect for her martyred husband, friends raised a fund in private gifts of $250,000 for her and her family.

At the request of her family a copy of Browning's poems was put in her hands in the exhibit of the costumes of the President's wives in the Smithsonian Institution, a fitting tribute to a highly educated woman. Her lavender satin dress is much admired and seems to go with her devotion to Browning and the American counterpart of the Victorian era.

CHESTER A. ARTHUR

1881–1885

Mary Arthur McElroy

CHESTER A. ARTHUR was born in Vermont in 1830, and died in New York in 1886. He was the twenty-first President of the United States, having succeeded to the Presidency when James A. Garfield died.

Chester Arthur was another widower President. He had lost his beautiful Southern wife before he came to the White House and he mourned deeply for her. He had two children and invited his widowed sister, Mary Arthur McElroy, to be Mistress of the White House during his term of office. She mothered his little boy and girl during her days in the White House and was a successful head of the house. She was well adapted to fill this position because of her tactful ways and her broad social experience. She and her brother dispensed graceful and dignified hospitality.

Chester Arthur and his sister were both unusually handsome in appearance. He is usually awarded the prize for good looks among the many fine looking Presidents. In her dress Mrs. McElroy was inclined to simplicity with elegance. Both she and her brother were light-hearted, sociable people, attractive and debonair. Chester Arthur had the first valet in the White House, which evidence of luxury disturbed the electorate as much as the habit of announcing visitors had upset an earlier era!

During the Arthur administration the White House was a cheery, sociable place with much entertaining and everything arranged on a generous scale—and in perfect taste. A more worldly atmosphere prevailed than in some previous administrations.

GROVER CLEVELAND

1885-1889
1893-1897

Frances Folsom Cleveland

GROVER CLEVELAND was the son of a minister who had nine children and an income of $600.00 a year. He was born in New Jersey in 1837. He practiced law in Buffalo; was sheriff of Erie County; Mayor of Buffalo; Governor of New York; President of the United States 1885-1889 and 1893-1897. He was the first Democratic President to be inaugurated in twenty-five years. When this bachelor President came to the White House, he invited his sister, Rose Cleveland, to be the official hostess, and she fulfilled her duties with quiet poise and dignity.

When it was learned that the popular bachelor President was to marry Frances Folsom, his ward, the beautiful twenty-one year old daughter of his former law partner, and a Wells College girl, every heart in the country was stirred by this story-book romance. Every press item about her was eagerly devoured. Mothers used her fidelity to her studies and her promptness in returning to college from her brief White House visits as shining examples for their daughters to emulate.

She was the first President's wife to be married in the White House, and the first one to have a child born there. These chapters in this thrilling romance of nation-wide interest softened for the time even the political asperities that had arisen over President Cleveland's startling monetary and tariff ideas, for "All the world loves a lover."

Mrs. Cleveland demonstrated the fact that a college education does not unfit a woman for domestic life, as was the popular notion of that day, when college was supposed to be the ruin of charm and practical virtues. Another erroneous assumption, that brains and beauty do not exist in the same feminine person, was definitely exploded. For Frances Folsom was one of the most beautiful women (in a wide field of beautiful women), who had ever adorned the White House. Her college education hadn't spoiled her face! She also destroyed another myth, that college women either had no children at all, or only averaged one and one-fourth child apiece—she had five whole children!

There was an interval of four years between the two Presidential terms of Grover Cleveland. Mrs. Cleveland was the idol of the entire country, and she and her family were welcomed back to the White House with joy! The testimony of every one about the White House in those days was to the effect that no more lovely woman in appearance and in spirit had ever before been a Mistress of the White House. An aura of romance continued to surround her until her death in December, 1947. As Mrs. Thomas Preston she lived in the midst of her family and friends in Princeton, New Jersey, in the dignity and ease that befitted her years and status. And history has already accorded her and her husband a high rank in the annals of White House families.

Courtesy—Library of Congress

LUCRETIA RUDOLPH GARFIELD

Courtesy—Library of Congress

FRANCES FOLSOM CLEVELAND

Courtesy—Library of Congress

CAROLINE SCOTT HARRISON

Courtesy—Library of Congress

IDA SAXTON McKINLEY

BENJAMIN HARRISON

1889–1893

Caroline Scott Harrison

THE DEMOCRATIC President Grover Cleveland was defeated in 1888 by the Republican Benjamin Harrison of Indiana, son of an Ohio farmer and a grandson of William Henry Harrison, who had been the ninth President of the United States. He was a graduate of Miami University; studied law; served as an officer in the Civil War; was United States Senator; and was elected to the Presidency in 1888.

Another college romance brought to the White House as First Lady Caroline Scott Harrison. Her father was President of Oxford College. She was a cultured and religious woman, a Presbyterian, and very musical and artistic. Having lived in social environments all of her life, Mrs. Harrison was very much at home in the White House. And as the wife of a United States Senator she had become well acquainted with Washington society. She continued to gather about her the old friends of other days, to engage actively in church work, and to have a great deal of joy in life, along with her exacting duties as Mistress of the White House.

President and Mrs. Harrison were well educated, accustomed to the best of society, and were wholly at ease wherever they were. They were sometimes said to be "home bodies," like President and Mrs. Hayes, though there was more gaiety around the White House under the Harrisons than during the Hayes family era, partially due to the presence of Mrs. Russell Harrison, Mrs. McKee, and Mrs. Dimmick, the latter who was Mrs. Harrison's niece.

Although at that time,—the early gay nineties,— evening gowns were very décolleté, Mrs. Harrison preferred to wear her dresses high in the neck; though there was a little concession made for the inaugural ball when a slight V shape at the throat was permitted. All this with an eye to the sensitivity of the electorate! Benjamin and Caroline Harrison were married before he was twenty-one years old. They dwelt together in peace and happiness for forty years. Her death in the White House toward the close of his administration cast a deep shadow over every one.

Mary Harrison McKee

1892–1893

Mary Harrison McKee, a widowed daughter, who had made her home with her parents at the White House, took over the management of this big establishment upon her mother's death. She and her mother had always been great friends and she deeply mourned her loss. Mary McKee is rightfully put in the category of the greatest White House beauties along with Dolly Madison, Lucy Hayes, and Frances Cleveland, for she was very beautiful. With her fine presence and cordial manners she made a host of friends.

There have often been extremes of joy and sorrow in the White House. Joy was brought to the remaining members of the family after Mrs. Harrison's death, by the rollicking children of Mrs. McKee. Baby McKee was especially dear to the President. There were many gay parties given for these children; and for the grown-ups there were the usual receptions and dinners, and more dances. The old East Room, which Mrs. John Adams long ago had been obliged to use as a drying room for the laundry, now echoed frequently with music and laughter of the young who turned the White House into a home. The first Christmas tree to be set up in the White House was under Benjamin Harrison's direction.

Mary Scott Lord Dimmick Harrison

Although never an actual mistress of the White House, Mrs. Dimmick, neé Mary Scott Lord, the attractive young widowed niece of Mrs. Benjamin Harrison, lived in the White House for two years until the death of her aunt, which occurred shortly before the close of President Harrison's term of office in 1893.

Mary Scott Lord grew up in Princeton, New Jersey. She married Walter Erskine Dimmick in 1881, who was attorney general in Pennsylvania in the 1870's. He died in 1882. After his death, Mrs. Dimmick made her home with her sister, wife of a naval officer in Annapolis, Maryland, and later with her mother in Washington, D.C. During that time she traveled considerably to interesting places. Then followed the very enjoyable two years in the White House with her aunt, where as a beautiful young widow she was the object of much attention and was one of the lively and beloved members of this fine White House family.

In 1893 she went to New York City and lived there until her marriage to ex-President Harrison in 1896 when she accompanied him to his former home in Indianapolis. They had one child, Elizabeth, a brilliant young woman, who became a member of the Bar and very prominent in the social and civic life of New York.

Mary Lord Harrison always lived a charmed life and was ever the center of an active, happy circle of her own family and friends. Benjamin Harrison was the leading counsel for Venezuela in the controversy between that country and England in 1898. During their stay of many months abroad at that time they were received like royalty by the crowned heads of Europe, and in every way measured up to their high station.

In 1901 ex-President Harrison died. After that Mrs. Harrison devoted herself largely to her daughter's education which included much foreign travel. After 1915 Mrs. Harrison resided in New York City. She was greatly interested in music and the fine arts, and in all matters concerning the federal government and the state. Her calendar for social and civic engagements was as crowded as a debutante's. Her youthful enthusiasms, her capacity for friendships and her keen interest in affairs made her extremely popular.

In 1940 she gave the old Harrison home in Indianapolis, Indiana, for a memorial to her husband, which is now called "The Benjamin Harrison Memorial Home." Mrs. Harrison died in New York on January 5, 1948.

WILLIAM McKINLEY

1897–1901

Ida Saxton McKinley

THE PARENTS of William McKinley were strong, plain, fine people who made great sacrifices that their nine children might be well educated. His father was an iron moulder, his mother, a farmer's daughter. The family were Scotch people who had settled in Pennsylvania and later moved to Ohio. They were earnest Methodists. Their son, William McKinley, worked very hard to help himself; he became a teacher; a lawyer; major in the Northern Army in the Civil War; went to Congress for fourteen years; was Governor of Ohio; and President.

Ida Saxton was the daughter of the leading banker of Canton, Ohio. She was educated largely in good private schools away from home and was the reigning belle of the town. Her father had made her cashier of his bank when she returned from a seven months' sojourn in Europe. She taught a Sunday School class, and was a very popular and prominent girl.

Upon her marriage to William McKinley, her

father gave them one of the finest houses in town as a wedding present. The death of their two children in infancy shocked Mrs. McKinley so deeply that she was always after that an invalid and given to frequent nervous attacks. Ida Saxton McKinley went to the White House with one of the most elaborate trousseaux of any of the White House women. Her clothes for the inaugural festivities are said to have cost $10,000. In the Smithsonian Museum collection in Washington is the gown she wore to the inaugural ball held March 4, 1897.

There was little of real gaiety in the White House during the McKinley regime because of Mrs. McKinley's precarious health; William McKinley's serious mind; and because of the bitter attacks launched against him by political rivals. These bitter attacks probably preyed on the mind of the crazed foreigner who shot the President in Buffalo at the Pan-American Exposition in 1901. Had there been children in the White House, the gloom might have lifted. But the Spanish-American War had cast its ugly shadow at this time over everything.

In view of her invalidism, Mrs. McKinley was always seated on her husband's right at dinners, and he did all in his power to conserve her strength. The McKinleys will go down in our annals as a charming, devoted couple, who made a real contribution to the upbuilding of home-life in America through their tenderness toward each other. His martyrdom, and her courageous spirit in the face of this dreadful tragedy, further enhanced the love of the nation for these two fine people who were a credit to our country, and who somehow typify the simplicity and soundness, and if one may say, the "*innocence* of 19th century domesticity!"

THEODORE ROOSEVELT

1901–1909

Edith Carow Roosevelt

THEODORE ROOSEVELT was born in New York in 1858. He became a Republican Assemblyman from New York; president of the New York Board of Police Commissioners; assistant secretary of the navy; Colonel of the First Volunteer Regiment (Rough Riders) in the Spanish American War; Governor of New York; Vice-president of the United States, and President upon the death of William McKinley; and elected President in 1904.

He was an author of high standing as well as a statesman. His literary prestige is as great as that of John Quincy Adams. His lively family have always been much liked—and like others of the tribe will go down in social history as among the champion talkers of all time.

The White House was at its very gayest when the Theodore Roosevelts were there. Probably the most brilliant of all White House weddings was that of the eldest daughter, Alice, to Nicholas Longworth in

1906. There had been eleven weddings in the historic Mansion before that one, but none that eclipsed it in the popularity of the "high contracting parties," as rural papers used to say.

Alice Roosevelt had been the first White House debutante for a long time. She has always been the object of much friendly interest, both because of her own interesting self and her apparently effortless inability to be inconspicuous. In her honor we still wear Alice blue. Her mother was lovely Alice Lee who came from a fine Southern family and who died when her daughter was born. Two years later, Theodore Roosevelt married Edith Carow who had been his playmate from childhood. She was a good mother to little Alice and to her own five children.

There was never a more united, joyous family than this Roosevelt family. They entertained crowds of relatives and friends, all rode together, walked, played games—all with the greatest joy—indeed with a sort of fury. Mrs. Roosevelt entered into all their many sports with zest. A day at Oyster Bay with the Roosevelts has been described as "like a circus only more dangerous."

Many-sided Theodore Roosevelt both in his public and his private life held up the highest and the best standards of American life. He was in many respects the most remarkable man ever to be President. There was something engaging, something electric about Theodore Roosevelt. He preached the merits of the "strenuous life," and was the best exponent of that life.

No other President and his wife has ever infused into the Executive Mansion such a spirit of gaiety, and unbounded welcome to people of all races and colors. This was an outward expression of an inner love of all their fellow human beings and an enthusiasm for life. Mrs. Roosevelt, too, led a strenuous life. She not only shared fully in all the physical and mental activities of her large family but she also quietly and efficiently kept up her tremendous household, family and social duties with poise and ease and with no loss of health, through all the seven years of her husband's presidency. She was always youthful, charming, vivacious.

The gown which Mrs. Roosevelt wore to her husband's inaugural ball has been placed in the collection in the National Museum. Because of its exquisite material, its graceful, beautiful lines, its ageless style, it is regarded by most observers as one of the most beautiful in that historic collection.

Mrs. Roosevelt was one of the finest of the women who have presided over the White House. To the manner born, the Theodore Roosevelts inherited from their forbears material wealth and had as second nature an instinctive courtesy and good will toward every one. Their good breeding was expressed in simplicity of conduct and life. Each of the children had his own duties and responsibilities, as well as his own interests and pursuits. Each had a definite plan of action each day. If the whole family did the same thing at the same time, as they often did, it was because of choice and because of their congeniality.

A cartoonist at the time of the death of Theodore Roosevelt caught the essence of his great spirit. He is pictured as a mounted Rough Rider ascending rapidly to the Heavens like Pegasus of old. He is waving his army hat in one hand and calls gallantly to those below, "So long!"

Mrs. Roosevelt lived until her death in September, 1948 in the old family home at Oyster Bay, Long Island, enjoying the abiding respect and affection of her family and of the whole nation.

WILLIAM HOWARD TAFT

1909–1913

Helen Herron Taft

HELEN HERRON did not meet her husband until she was eighteen years old, though they were both born and brought up in Cincinnati and their parents were friends. She was the daughter of John William Herron, a graduate of Miami University, in the days when Benjamin Harrison was also a student there. Her mother was the daughter of a member of Congress from New York State, an able and brilliant woman endowed with a keen sense of humor, a nimble wit, and was the mother of eleven children.

It is said that Helen Herron resembled her unusual mother in many respects. She specialized in music in her youth and carried this interest with her through her life. She taught school for two years. Later with two of her most intimate friends she started a "Salon" for the discussion of serious matters like politics, economics, education, etc. Among the favored few young men invited to this select circle of brilliant people were William and Horace Taft.

William Howard Taft rose rapidly in his profession as a lawyer. He was a member of the Supreme Court of Ohio; Solicitor General of the United States; a Judge of the Federal Circuit Court; Chairman of the Civil Commission to investigate conditions in the Philippines, where he helped to restore law and order, and became their first civil Governor; Minister of War in President Theodore Roosevelt's Cabinet; and President of the United States. Later he was made Chief Justice of the Supreme Court. He served in that capacity until he resigned in 1930, shortly before his death.

The William Tafts were a happy and united family. They could laugh at themselves and at such incidents as the one about a dull dowager who said to Judge Taft at a dinner party shortly after he returned from his long sojourn in the Philippines, (which had been much publicized), that she did hope he would take a trip to the Philippines some day, for friends had told her it was such a quaint place and she was sure Judge Taft would enjoy it. And there was another woman who said to Mrs. Taft, when her husband was in the Cabinet, "How sorry you must have been to leave the Philippines where you were a *Queen,* and come here where you are a *nobody."*

Mrs. Taft was an unusually successful hostess at the White House. She was kind, gracious, attractive in appearance, and always beautifully and appropriately clothed. She was one of the most active of the President's wives with her many cultural and charitable pursuits. It was she who was instrumental in establishing band concerts on certain afternoons along the Speedway, thereby giving freely to every one the advantages of hearing good music well played.

Always devoted to the fine arts and to enjoyment of interesting people, her receptions and entertainments were delightful. Domesticity was her second nature. Her husband, her children and their interests were never neglected. Mrs. Taft was instrumental in beautifying the White House gardens, and then proceeded to use them. She arranged the garden parties held on the White House lawn, where people from every walk of life could be guests of the President's family. And she planned the cherry blossom rows along the Potomac River.

The Tafts entertained well and generously. Their three lively children were very popular. Mrs. Taft put the front door attendants in livery, which was a great improvement over the former practice of having forbidding looking policemen receive the callers and their cards. Mrs. Taft also engaged a house-keeper who did the routine work and kept the accounts. President Taft's salary and entertainment funds had been increased at that time, so the suppers accompanying receptions were resumed and more formality became possible.

The most important event of Mrs. Taft's four years in the White House was the celebration of their twenty-fifth wedding anniversary. This took the form of a great garden party when several thousands of people crowded into the White House and its garden.

The death in 1930 of Judge Taft added Mrs. Taft to the list of widows of former Presidents—a widowhood from which she was released by death in 1943. Her husband always affirmed that his eminence and his happy, successful life was due to his devoted and intelligent wife.

Courtesy—Library of Congress

EDITH CAROW ROOSEVELT

Courtesy—Library of Congress

HELEN HERRON TAFT

Courtesy—Library of Congress

EDITH BOLLING GALT WILSON

Courtesy—Library of Congress

FLORENCE KLING HARDING

WOODROW WILSON

1913–1921

Ellen Axson Wilson

No MAN ever became President of the United States with a more scholarly background than did Woodrow Wilson. He studied law and politics at the University of Virginia; tried to develop a law practice in Atlanta; wrote books on government and politics; became a college professor at several colleges; finally the President of Princeton; then Governor of New Jersey, and finally President of the United States.

The first Mrs. Wilson brought to the White House all the grace, charm and beauty of person and character which she had inherited and acquired from her good Southern and Presbyterian ancestry. Ellen Lou Axson Wilson was a wise and devoted wife and mother. She had three talented daughters.

The Wilsons were a devoted family,—some said they were aloof socially,—but they were merely selective of their friends and not gregarious. None of the family seemed to regard the White House as a public place but rather as their own home during their residence in it. "No one was ever invited to the White House in the eight years they lived there for political purposes," said David Lawrence.

The Wilsons were gracious at the official affairs they had to give in the White House but they did not unbend as on more informal occasions among their own friends. The Wilson girls were brought up in the same Puritanical surroundings that their parents had known. Music, art, literature and the drama furnished general entertainment, while church and social work attracted their special interest. President Wilson canceled the usual inaugural ball because he thought it was a useless extravagance.

Mrs. Wilson did much to improve the housing conditions of Washington. Her quiet influence was a powerful factor in her husband's successful life. Ellen Axson Wilson lived only a year and a half in the White House, but she left many beautiful touches there and in the gardens as evidences of her love of beauty and her creative ability. She was very charitable. On her deathbed she was cheered by news that Congress had passed a bill in which she was greatly concerned because it affected the welfare of those who needed help. She fitted up the Blue Mountain Room in the White House with handiwork of the poor but artistic women living back in the Blue Ridge Mountains. Her memory was tenderly cherished by her daughters and a wide circle of devoted relatives and friends.

Edith Bolling Galt Wilson

A year after his wife's death, Wilson's romance with charming, widowed Edith Bolling Galt, an attractive Southerner, resulted in their marriage. This second happy marriage seemed to give him new zest for life. The second Mrs. Wilson succeeded Miss Margaret Wilson as the nation's hostess. She is a quiet, gracious woman who devoted herself to the care of her husband to the end of his life in 1924. She had apparently no selfish aspirations for personal social success, thereby enhancing the already highly respected status which she enjoyed in Washington previous to her marriage. During her husband's last illness the gates of the White House were closed. She is now (1949) living in quiet dignity in the nation's Capitol.

The dress of beautiful material on the wax figure of Edith Bolling Wilson in the National Museum is one that she wore to several important Court functions in Europe when she was with President Wilson at the close of the First World War. This dress was one of her trousseau gowns that, in keeping with wartime economy, had been made over three times before the First Lady wore it abroad.

WARREN GAMALIEL HARDING

1921–1923

Florence Kling Harding

"BABBITT HAS moved into the White House," was said of Warren Harding. He said of himself, in his unaffected Middle Western manner, that he was "just folks." He had known only hard work from childhood. Post-war times were so bad that there was no parade, no inaugural ball, no brilliant celebration to mark his inaugural.

Florence Kling, the daughter of a banker, the richest man in Marion, Ohio, was left a widow at the age of eighteen years with a small son. She married Warren Harding in spite of her father's opposition. Mrs. Harding helped her husband loyally at every point in his life, and was generally acknowledged to be the quiet force which put him in the White House. She went down to the office of her husband's paper to help in an emergency for several days and remained for fourteen years. She took charge of the carriers, the circulation departments and made them pay.

When she went to the White House to live, though

her health was not good, she entered with fine spirit into all her duties there and helped her husband in countless ways. At their first New Year's reception, which lasted from eleven in the morning to five in the afternoon, they stood in line during those six hours and shook hands with many thousands of people from all over the nation. At the close of this affair Mrs. Harding's hands were so swollen that her gloves had to be cut from her hands.

Mrs. Harding entered into many forms of educational and social welfare activities. In her quiet, efficient way she accomplished a great deal of good. Her simplicity and directness appealed to young people and they knew she understood and loved them. A citizen of Marion, Ohio, said of her, "She is nice to everybody, knows how to run things, too. Runs her house; runs the paper if necessary; runs Warren; runs everything but the car, and she could run that if she wanted to. Florence is all right, she is."

Florence Harding was a woman too big for any petty resentments, which was demonstrated when the committee in charge of installing the figures of the President's wives in the National Museum showed her that her figure had been placed in the same case with that of Edith Bolling Wilson. Their husbands were not friends. Her response was, "How happy I am to know that I am to be in the same case with that lovely woman."

In the midst of all the senseless, cruel gossip and slander which was vented upon the dead President and upon his suffering widow, we must in justice to this blameless woman recall her as the ever devoted wife who was reading aloud to her husband when Death took him.

CALVIN COOLIDGE

1923–1929

Grace Goodhue Coolidge

SINCE THE passing away of the old aristocratic regime in the time of John Quincy Adams no other administration marks the end of an era as distinctly as that of Coolidge. The 1920's were unique in American life and so, as an American type, was Calvin Coolidge —a silent, sober "Yankee" from head to foot. In William Allen White's "Life of Coolidge" he says of him at one period—"he deliberately, quietly, soberly married and he chose well—a teacher in the Clark School for the Deaf—accustomed to silence—Miss Grace Goodhue, a Vermonter, a splendid woman, vivacious, highly intuitive, charming and beautiful."

She was his complement in every way. The two made a full team. "A man who is wise in the affairs of the heart need not fear folly in the affairs of the head." Calvin Coolidge's grandfather, a very silent man, said to Calvin's father, "Cal don't say much." "No, he ain't gabby," was the response. To what extent Mrs. Coolidge influenced her husband's judgments only two persons may testify. One was too silent to say and the other was too smart!

More anecdotes probably hinge on the conversational brevity of "silent Cal" than on any president since Lincoln. Apropos of Mrs. Coolidge teaching in the Deaf School a wit said, "Having taught the deaf to hear she may now inspire the dumb to speak."

Mrs. Coolidge was a typical American woman in that she had done her own work, reared her own family, and lived a simple life with an honest man. Many people felt that without Mrs. Coolidge her husband would not have climbed to such heights. When they came to the White House they brought their two fine young sons to whom they had taught the value of honesty, truthfulness and valor. The death of one of their two sons during their first year in the White House aroused the sympathy of the nation, and nearly crushed his parents. But they bore their sorrow with restraint and did not allow any private grief to interfere with their public duty.

In placing the handsome gown belonging to Mrs. Coolidge in the National Museum, she pinned on the lovely soft velvet tiered dress her Greek letter fraternity pin of Pi Beta Phi, for her loyalties are deep and enduring.

Mrs. Coolidge is now (1949) living in Northampton in the serenity and dignity that well befits this former Mistress of the White House.

Courtesy—Library of Congress

GRACE GOODHUE COOLIDGE

Courtesy—Library of Congress

LOU HENRY HOOVER

Courtesy—Library of Congress

ELEANOR ROOSEVELT ROOSEVELT

Courtesy—Library of Congress

BESS WALLACE TRUMAN

HERBERT HOOVER

1929–1932

Lou Henry Hoover

HERBERT HOOVER was born in 1874 in West Branch, Iowa, of fine pioneer Quaker stock. His forbears had over a period of several generations gone from Philadelphia to Maryland, thence to North Carolina before the Revolution; then on to Ohio, across to Iowa, and he in his early youth went to Oregon. The Hoover family were truly pioneers. It was mainly the younger sons of each generation who pushed further on to adventure and settlement in the new frontiers of their times.

Wherever the Hoovers went they took an active part in creating a new Quaker settlement, a new community, a new focus of human habitation. The center of this new settlement was always a Friends' Meetinghouse, a school, and a village of Friends. It was to such a Quaker settlement in Newberg, Oregon that the young orphan, Herbert Hoover, journeyed in his boyhood to live with his uncle, Dr. John Minthorn, then President of Pacific Friends Academy (later

Pacific College). From there he entered Stanford University in 1891. He was the first student to take up residence there; he was graduated in 1895; and became its most distinguished alumnus.

While at Stanford University he met Lou Henry of Monterey, California, a young and beautiful girl, who was deeply interested in geology and kindred subjects, as he was. They were married in 1899 at her home in Monterey. Then they journeyed over most of the world together wherever his profession of mining engineering took him. Wherever they went they were followed by many friends with whom they always developed an interesting and helpful life.

Mr. Hoover came into the Presidency as the first World Citizen to hold this post, and one who after having been for many years past a notably successful mining engineer, took up the broader fields of public service. The Hoovers always gave liberally of themselves and of all their resources to each community where they dwelt. That spirit of helpfulness was manifested to a high degree in Washington, D.C.

No other First Lady was ever better fitted to enter the White House than was Lou Henry Hoover. No other First Lady was ever more socially experienced or more finely equipped. With good health and strength, a calm spirit, and great intellectual vigor, her leadership and womanly quality was recognized by every one. Tall, statuesque and poised, Mrs. Hoover presided over state and private functions with an easy grace seldom equaled by any one else in Washington.

Their two fine sons and grandchildren are the special joy of Herbert Hoover, the only living ex-President of the United States. He is everywhere acknowledged as the world's greatest humanitarian.

The crowds at the White House on the inauguration day of President Hoover were like some huge mass meeting. Upwards of eighteen hundred luncheon guests were at the White House that March 4, 1929. Among the fifteen hundred guests at tea at the White House that afternoon were the governors and their staffs from all the states.

Of all the White House families in history the Hoovers were the most distinguished for the number and variety of their guests and the many types of entertainments. White House staff members never knew how many guests would be asked at the last minute for meals, for the Hoovers were always surrounded by a crowd of devoted friends from every part of the world. Their home at Palo Alto, California, was for many years the center of friendly gatherings and visits from distinguished people from all over the world who sought out this most devoted and brilliant couple.

Not since Theodore Roosevelt's day has there been a President and his wife with so many varied interests, with so sincere a desire to be helpful, and with such complete domestic felicity.

Something of the tenderness and understanding of childhood, which both Mr. and Mrs. Hoover had, was expressed by President Hoover in 1930 before the 1200 delegates to the White House conference on

Child Health and Protection, when he said, "We approach all problems of childhood with affection. Theirs is the province of joy and good humor. They are the most wholesome of the race for they are fresher from God. We envy them the freshness of adventure and discovery of life; we mourn over the disappointments they will meet."

Mrs. Hoover often said that she had no taste for a career on her own account, and that her outside interests were especially with the Girl Scouts and other such character building agencies. Hers was not by any means a passive nature, but a very gentle one coupled with firmness—truly a many-sided, beautiful nature. She was a gentlewoman, a true friend, a real patriot. The whole nation shared in the sorrow which her family felt at her death in 1944.

FRANKLIN DELANO ROOSEVELT

1932-1945

Eleanor Roosevelt Roosevelt

WITH THE white light of publicity beating so mercilessly and so constantly upon Eleanor Roosevelt and her late husband; and with her frequent public appearances in person, in radio and in print, we must all have the feeling that we know Mrs. Franklin D. Roosevelt personally or that we did know her in a previous existence. She is approachable, very energetic, cordial, and a leader, a thorough Roosevelt, having been born a Roosevelt and having married one of that vigorous family. She is the first "career woman" to have presided over the White House.

Noting her tireless energy and her fund of ideas, makes one wonder if the gloomy predictions of some elderly Jeremiahs may not come true that a woman will some day be not only Mistress of the White House but President of the United States as well. Countless American women carry on active professional or business lives, keep house well, and rear families, all at the same time. It does not stretch the imagination too greatly to reflect that such a superwoman may some day hold the highest office in the land.

But this reflection is not born of wishful thinking. Many of us are sufficiently old-fashioned to prefer to live not under a matriarchy nor yet under a patriarchy, but to have equal responsibilities and privileges with men, with the ablest person in the United States as President.

We are too close to the Franklin Roosevelts to have any perspective or to put any fair valuation upon them. We do know that they were justly very popular in the White House; that they came of an old American family who have played their full part in the upbuilding of the country.

Whether progressive forces that have always been operating through a steady process of evolution are better than arriving at changes through revolutionary methods is best, no one now can say. But at least we are all united in a common love of our country, and a determination to keep it free.

Eleanor Roosevelt is one of our outstanding women. Like some of the other members of the Roosevelt family she is extremely versatile and has their great physical vigor. As a writer, radio commentator, hostess to the most distinguished people of the whole world during her long sojourn in the White House, delegate to the United Nations, and sponsor of many important national movements, she still moves across the stage of events as a striking personality and a woman of great influence.

HARRY S. TRUMAN

1945–

Bess Wallace Truman

UPON THE sudden death in April, 1945 of President Franklin Delano Roosevelt, Vice-president Harry S. Truman, former United States Senator from Missouri, became President of the United States.

He and his wife, Bess Truman, and their young daughter, Margaret, moved to the White House from their modest apartment in Washington where the women had done their own work and had lived quietly. With the adaptability which is characteristic of Americans, the Truman trio fitted into its new home and new roles with dignity and ease. Margaret attended George Washington University and studied vocal music when her father was a senator, and Mrs. Truman was one of his secretaries.

In the 1948 election President Truman was elected president in his own right.

Mrs. Truman seems destined to become, like many of her predecessors, a successful and agreeable First Lady. She has studiously avoided the lime light; has held no press conferences; has arranged White House entertainments with simplicity; has manifested her sincere interest in music and other arts; is a good housekeeper and home-maker; and has a real capacity for friendships. Their young daughter, Margaret, has the same deep interest in music which President Truman has. She has talent and the quality of mind which makes her persevere for perfection in the field of vocal music. She is altogether an admirable young woman and a worthy President's daughter.

Six weeks after his return from World War I (June, 1919), Harry Truman married Bess Wallace, school-teacher daughter of a farmer and the granddaughter of a well-known flour miller. She is said to be the only girl he ever cared for. She was the lively, attractive little blond girl who had in childhood attended the same Presbyterian Sunday School that he did.

Mrs. Truman when queried by press women recently, answered that she considered the greatest asset of a president's wife to be good health and a well-developed sense of humor; she does not think there will ever be a woman president; she keeps scrap books for President Truman and Margaret, but not for herself; she does not find White House entertaining a task; she wants to return to Independence, Missouri, when her husband is no longer President.

Mrs. Truman served in the U.S.O. during the war; she has organized a Spanish class which meets regularly once a week in the White House, the other students being wives of Army and Navy officers, Supreme

Court Judges, Cabinet officers, Senators, et al. Mrs. Truman takes this class seriously as she does everything else she undertakes, and it is said she appears at this class always with her "home work" well prepared. Her loyalty to her Missouri home bridge club and the memorable meeting they had at the White House attests her loyalty to relatives and old friends, who undoubtedly outrank newer and more nationally prominent ones in her affections.

A writer in the New York *Times* recently said of Bess Wallace Truman, "She is a real person pursuing a stable pattern of her own design." She is so much an individualist that she would be stepping out of character if she tried to be like any other woman who had ever before lived in the White House. For five generations her highly respected family have lived in Independence, Missouri. Mrs. Truman reflects that solidarity and assurance that comes from such a stable background in the quietness and dignity with which she has stepped into the role of the current Mistress of the White House.

Epilogue

THE PROCESSION of First Ladies of America that has just passed before our view reveals a uniformly high quality of womanly character, intelligence, and patriotism. True to the American way of life, our Presidents and our First Ladies have come from every social strata. Each First Lady has measured up to her high responsibility. Each has played her part in shaping in her time the high destiny of America.

With the memory of these noble women of the past we are inspired to abiding faith that our country will continue always to enjoy a representative form of government and that in all matters of defense from enemies within and without that the "Mistresses of the White House," and all of us, will measure up to our high privilege as citizens of this great nation.

We say together devoutly,

> "Lord God of Hosts, whose mighty hand
> Dominion holds on sea and land,
> In peace and war Thy will we see
> Shaping the larger liberty;
> Nations may rise and nations fall,
> Thy changeless purpose rules them all."

Epilogue

The Narrator recites the lines of "America, the Beautiful—"

O beautiful for spacious skies,
For amber waves of grain,
For purple mountain majesties
Above the fruited plain.
America! America! God shed His grace on thee,
And crown thy good with brotherhood
From sea to shining sea.

O beautiful for pilgrim feet
Whose stern impassioned stress
A thoroughfare for freedom beat
Across the wilderness.
America! America! God mend thine ev'ry flaw,
Confirm thy soul in self-control,
Thy liberty in law.

O beautiful for heroes proved
In liberating strife,
Who more than self their country loved,
And mercy more than life.
America! America! May God thy gold refine
Till all success be nobleness
And ev'ry gain divine.

O beautiful for patriot dream
That sees beyond the years
Thine alabaster cities gleam
Undimmed by human tears.

America! America! God shed His grace on thee,
And crown thy good with brotherhood
From sea to shining sea.

Then the entire audience rises and sings this song in conclusion.

As the audience, led by voices in the wings, sings "America, the Beautiful," the procession files off the stage while the lights are slowly dimmed. Martha Washington slowly leads the procession and the last to leave the stage is Bess Truman. The song ends in semi-darkness.

Bibliography

Adams, Abigail. *Letters.* (Ed. by Charles Francis Adams.) Hurd & Houghton, 1875.
Adams, James Truslow. *The Living Jefferson.* Scribner, 1931.
Agar, Herbert. *The People's Choice, from Washington to Harding.* Houghton Mifflin & Company, 1933.
Anderson, Mary Frances. An Article on "The Costumes of the Mistresses of the White House." Vol. XXIII —4th Quarter, No. 4 Americana, Oct. 1929.
Anonymous. "First Ladies of Other Years." *N.Y. Times,* Feb. 7, 1937.
Anonymous. "Obituary, Hannah Van Buren." *Albany Argus,* Feb. 8, 1819.
Armstrong, Margaret. *Five Generations.* Harper, 1930.
Beard, C. A. *The Presidents in American History.* J. Messuer, Inc., 1946.
Biographical Sketches of Our National Presidents and Ladies of the White House. Lincoln, Nebr., Lincoln School Supply Co., 1932. 2 pts. in IV.
Bobbe, Dorothie. *Abigail Adams, the Second First Lady.* New York, Minton, Balch & Co., 1929. 336 pp. "The President's House": pp. 304–307.
Bowers, Claude. *The Tragic Era.* Literary Guild, 1929.
Bradford, Gamaliel. *Wives-.* Harper & Bros., 1925.
Bradford, Gamaliel. *Portraits of American Women.* Houghton Mifflin & Co., 1919.
Briggs, Emily E. *The Olivia Letters, Being Some History of Washington City for Forty Years as Told by the*

Letters of a Newspaper Correspondent. New York and Washington, The Neale Publishing Company, 1906. 445 pp. Pp. 55–58, 121–125, 168–172, 256–261, 388–395, 430–434.

Brooks, Geraldine. *Dames and Daughters of Colonial Days, 1731–1802.* Thomas Y. Crowell Pub. Co., 1900.

Busbey, Mrs. Katherine (Graves). "Mrs. Taft's Home-Making." *Good Housekeeping,* Sept. 1911, v. 53: 290–298.

Cavanagh, Frances. *Children of the White House.* New York, Chicago, Rand, McNally & Co. (1936). 35 pp.

Chittenden, Cecil R. *The White House and Its Yesterdays;* a narrative of an American home. Alexandria, Va., Washington–Mt. Vernon Memorial Book Corporation (1932). 155 pp.

Colman, Edna Mary. *Seventy-Five Years of White House Gossip.* New York, Doubleday, Page & Co., 1926.

Colman, Edna Mary. *White House Gossip from Andrew Johnson to Calvin Coolidge.* New York, Doubleday, Page & Co., 1927.

Coolidge, Grace A. (Goodhue). "Mrs. Calvin Coolidge." "Making Ourselves at Home in the White House." *American Magazine,* v. 108. Nov. 1929. "Home Again." *American Magazine,* v. 109, Jan. 1930: 18–19.

Court Circles of the Republic. Hartford Pub. Co., 1869.

Crook, William H. *Memories of the White House.* Subtitle, *The Home Life of Our Presidents from Lincoln to Theodore Roosevelt.* Comp. and ed. by Henry Rood. Boston, Little, Brown and Co., 1911. 308 pp.

Cunningham, A. S. *Everything You Want to Know About the Presidents.*

Curtis, G. T. *Biography of James Buchanan, Including Letters.* Harper, 1883.

Dean, Elizabeth L. *Dolly Madison, the Nation's Hostess.* Boston, Lathrop, Lee & Shepard Co. (1928). 250 pp. See Index under President's House.
Desmond, Alice C. *Martha Washington, Our First Lady.* Dodd, Mead, 1942.
Ellet, Elizabeth F. L. *Women of the American Revolution,* 1850; Jacobs (reprint) 1900. *Pioneer Women of the West.* New York, Scribner, 1854.
"First Ladies of the Land, Past and Present." *Literary Digest,* v. 85, May 9, 1925: 36–38.
Fox, Frances Margaret. *Washington, D.C., the Nation's Capital, Romance—Adventure—Achievement;* a book for young people. New York, Chicago, Rand McNally & Co. (1929). 370 pp. Pp. 23–31, 79–84, 337–345.
Garland, Hamlin. *A Daughter of the Middle Border.* Macmillan, 1921.
Gerry, Margarita Spalding, ed. *Andrew Johnson in the White House; Being Reminiscences of William H. Crook.* Century, Sept.–Oct. 1908, v. 76: 653–669, 863–877.
Godey, Louis A. *The Lady's Book* (magazine), 1836–1846.
Hamilton, Holman. *Life of Zachary Taylor.* Bobbs-Merrill, 1891.
Hampton, Vernon B. *Religious Background of the White House.* Boston, The Christopher Publishing House, 1932. 416 pp.
Hanaford, Phebe. *Daughters of America.* Russell, 1883.
Haskins Service. *Our Presidents and Their Wives.* Washington, D.C. Rev. edition, 1947. (Copies of this booklet may be had for 20¢ each. Send coin, carefully wrapped in paper, giving name and complete address and stating the title of the booklet desired. Address: The Haskins Service, Washington 2, D.C.)

Hayes, Rutherford B. *In the White House; Reminiscences of William H. Crook.* Century, Mar. 1909, v. 77: 643–665.
Helm, Katherine. *The True Story of Mary, Wife of Lincoln.* New York and London, Harper & Brothers, publishers, 1928. 309 pp. See Index under White House.
Hoes, Laurence G. "Mrs. Hoover's Gift to History." White House parlor that once was private parlor of Mrs. James Monroe restored. *Sunday Star,* Washington, D.C., Nov. 6, 1932, pt. 2, p. 1: 3–6.
Hoes, Rose Gouverneur. *The Dresses of the Mistresses of the White House as Shown in the U.S. National Museum.* 3rd edition, 1931. American Historical Society. The Historical Publishing Co., 1931. (Order from Mr. Laurence G. Hoes, 6115 Western Avenue, Washington, D.C. $1 a copy.)
Hoover, Irwin H. *Forty-Two Years in the White House.* Boston and New York, Houghton Mifflin Co. (1934). 332 pp.
Irelan, John Robert. *History of the Life, Administration and Times of Martin Van Buren.* Fairbanks & Palmer, 1886–89.
Irelan, John Robert. *Life, Administration and Times of Franklin Pierce.* Fairbanks & Palmer, 1888.
Jaffray, Mrs. Elizabeth. *Secrets of the White House . . . Housekeeper from the Days of Taft to Coolidge.* New York, Cosmopolitan Book Corporation, 1927. 200 pp.
James, Marquis: *Andrew Jackson.* Bobbs-Merrill, 1937.
Jefferson, Thomas. *Letters.* (Ed. by J. G. Hamilton.) Houghton Mifflin Co., 1926.
Kane, Joseph N. *Famous First Facts; a record of first happenings, discoveries and inventions in the United*

States. New York, The H. W. Wilson Co., 1933. 757 pp.
Keckley, Elizabeth. *Behind the Scenes.* Carleton, 1868.
(Langford), Mrs. Laura (Carter) Holloway. *The Ladies of the White House; or, In the Home of the Presidents.* Philadelphia, Bradley & Co., 1881–1882–1884.
Leech, Margaret. *Reveille in Washington.* Harper & Brothers, 1941.
Lewis, Ethel. *The White House.* Dodd Mead & Co., 1937.
Logan, Mary S. (Cunningham) "Mrs. J. A. Logan." *Our National Government; or, Life and Scenes in Our National Capital.* Minneapolis, Minn., H. L. Baldwin Co., publishers (1908). 770 pp. Published in 1901, under title *Thirty Years in Washington.* . . .
Looker, Earle. *The White House Gang.* New York, Chicago, Fleming H. Revell Co. (1929). 244 pp.
McAdoo, Mrs. Eleanor Randolph (Wilson) *The Woodrow Wilsons.* New York, The Macmillan Co., 1937. 301 pp. "The White House": pp. 200–301.
McKim and the White House. Personal reminiscences of Charles Follen McKim. Architectural record, Jan. 1916, v. 39: 84–88.
Madison, Dorothea. *Life and Letters.* (Ed. by her great-niece, L. B. Cutts, 1851.) Houghton Mifflin (reprint) 1886.
Martineau, Harriet. *Society in America: A Retrospect of Western Travel.* Saunders & Otley (London), 1838.
Milhollen and Kaplan, *Presidents on Parade,* The Macmillan Company, 1948.
Minnigerode, Meade. *Some American Ladies.* G. P. Putnam Sons, 1926.
Monroe, James. *Unpublished Letters and Papers.* New York Public Library.
Montgomery, Henry. *Life of William Henry Harrison.*

Winston, 1852. Suffolk County Maps and Records. Long Island Historical Society.
Moore, Frank. *Women of the War*. Scranton, 1866.
Moran, T. F. *American Presidents*. New York, Thomas Y. Crowell Co., 1928.
Morgan, James. *Our Presidents*. New York, The Macmillan Co., 1928.
Morrow, Honore Wilsie. *Mary Todd Lincoln*. Morrow, 1928.
Nevins, Allan. *American Social History*. Holt, 1923.
"Presidents and First Ladies; White House Manners and Customs." *Ladies' Home Journal*, v. 53, May, 1936: 8–9, June: 16–17, July: 14–15, Aug.: 14.
Queens of American Society. Porter & Coates, 1867.
Randall, H. S. *Life of Thomas Jefferson*. Lippincott, 1871.
Randolph, Mary. *Presidents and First Ladies*. New York, London, D. Appleton–Century Co., Inc., 1936. 257 pp.
Randolph, Sarah N. *Domestic Life of Thomas Jefferson*. Cambridge U. Press (reprint), 1939.
Royce, Sarah. *A Frontier Lady*. Yale U. Press, 1933.
Sage, Agnes Carolyn. *The Boys and Girls of the White House*. New York, F. A. Stokes Co. (1909). 326 pp.
Sandburg, Carl, and Paul Angle. *Mary Lincoln, Wife and Widow*. Harcourt Brace, 1932.
Selden, Charles A. "Six White House Wives and Widows." *Ladies' Home Journal*, v. 44, June, 1927: 18–19.
Singleton, Esther. *The Story of the White House*. Vols. 1 and 2, New York, The McClure Company, 1907.
Smith, Bessie White. *The Romances of the Presidents*. Lathrop, Lee & Co., 1932.
Smith, Margaret Bayard. *Forty Years of Washington Society*. Scribner (reprint), 1906.
Stephenson, Sam C. *Biographical Sketches of Our Na-*

tional Presidents and the Ladies of the White House. Lincoln, Nebr., Lincoln School Supply Co., 1932. 2 pts. in 1 v.

Stern, Elizabeth G. "Exacting Role of the First Lady." *N.Y. Times,* Mar. 14, 1937.

Sweetser, Kate Dickinson. *Famous Girls of the White House.* Rev. ed. New York, Thomas Y. Crowell Co. (1937). 303 pp.

"The New White House." *Harper's Weekly,* July 14, 1906, v. 50: 989–993, 1003.

Tyler, Lyon Gardiner. *Letters and Times of the Tylers.* Whittet & Shepperson, 1884.

U.S. Library of Congress. Division of Bibliography. Biographies of the Presidents of the United States: a bibliographical list. Compiled by Grace Hadley Fuller under the direction of Florence S. Hellman, Chief Bibliographer. (Washington, D.C.) 1937. 49 pp. Mimeographed.

Van Buren, Martin. *Autobiography.* American Historical Association, Vol. II, 1918.

Whipple, Wayne. *The Story of the White House and Its Home Life.* Completed by Alice Roosevelt Longworth. Boston, Mass., Dwinell-Wright Co., 1937. 62 pp.

Whitton, Mary Ormsbee. *First First Ladies, 1789–1865.* A study of the wives of the early presidents. Hastings House, 1948.

Winton, Robert. *Andrew Johnson, Plebeian and Patriot.* Holt, 1928.

Woolfall, Lila Graham Alliger. *Presiding Ladies of the White House.* Washington, Bureau of National Literature and Art (1903). 137 pp. Published 1898 under title: *A Pocket History of the Ladies of the White House,* by Olga Stanley (pseud.)

The World Almanac 1950.

Wright, Richardson. *Forgotten Ladies*. Lippincott, 1928.

For the most complete bibliography available up to 1939, the year of its publication, the reader should consult "The White House." A biographical list compiled by Ann Duncan Brown under the direction of Florence S. Hellman, Chief Biographer of The Library of Congress, Washington, D.C.

Publications by American Historical Society.
"Dictionary of American Biography."
"Dictionary of American History."

And many other sources of material were found in old books (often out of print); indexed magazine articles; old documents, letters, and conversations with members of the families of more recent presidents, and descendants of those of the past.

It has been suggested to the author that some of the groups who produce this pageant might care to avail themselves of vocal or instrumental music throughout the Narrator's Tale, either in the form of interludes or to be performed during the entrance or exit of the various characters from the stage.

A considerable amount of music of patriotic character is available and the following works of reference are recommended for this purpose:

The American Song Bag, Carl Sandburg, New York, Harcourt Brace & Co.

Stories of Our American Patriotic Songs, Dr. John Henry Lyons, New York, The Vanguard Press.

History Sings, Hazel Gertrude Kinscella, Lincoln, Nebraska, The University Publishing Company.

Presidents of the United States

George Washington *	1789–1797
John Adams	1797–1801
Thomas Jefferson *	1801–1809
James Madison *	1809–1817
James Monroe *	1817–1825
John Quincy Adams	1825–1829
Andrew Jackson *	1829–1837
Martin Van Buren	1837–1841
William Henry Harrison	1841
John Tyler	1841–1845
James Knox Polk	1845–1849
Zachary Taylor	1849–1850
Millard Fillmore	1850–1853
Franklin Pierce	1853–1857
James Buchanan	1857–1861
Abraham Lincoln *	1861–1865
Andrew Johnson	1865–1869
Ulysses Grant *	1869–1877
Rutherford B. Hayes	1877–1881
James Garfield	1881
Chester Alan Arthur	1881–1885
Grover Cleveland *	1885–1889; 1893–1897
Benjamin Harrison	1889–1893
William McKinley *	1897–1901
Theodore Roosevelt *	1901–1909

* Indicates two terms.
** Indicates more than two terms.

William Howard Taft	1909–1913
Woodrow Wilson *	1913–1921
Warren G. Harding	1921–1923
Calvin Coolidge	1923–1929
Herbert C. Hoover	1929–1932
Franklin D. Roosevelt **	1932–1945
Harry S. Truman	1945–

* Indicates two terms.
** Indicates more than two terms.

Mistresses of the White House

Martha Dandridge Washington	1789–1797
Abigail Smith Adams	1797–1801
Martha Jefferson Randolph Martha Wayles Jefferson	1801–1809
Dolly Payne Madison	1809–1817
Elizabeth Kortright Monroe	1817–1825
Louisa Catherine Johnson Adams	1825–1829
Rachel Donelson Jackson Emily Donelson	1829–1837
Sarah Angelica Van Buren	1837–1841
Anna Symmes Harrison	1841
Letitia Christian Tyler Julia Gardiner Tyler	1841–1845
Sarah Childress Polk	1845–1849
Margaret Smith Taylor	1849–1850
Abigail Powers Fillmore Mary Abigail Fillmore	1850–1853
Jane Appleton Pierce	1853–1857
Harriet Lane Johnston	1857–1861
Mary Todd Lincoln	1861–1865
Eliza McCardle Johnson	1865–1869
Julia Dent Grant	1869–1877
Lucy Webb Hayes	1877–1881
Lucretia Rudolph Garfield	1881–
Mary Arthur McElroy	1881–1885
Frances Folsom Cleveland	1885–1889; 1893–1897

Caroline Scott Harrison Mary Harrison McKee	1889–1893
Ida Saxton McKinley	1897–1901
Edith Carow Roosevelt	1901–1909
Helen Herron Taft	1909–1913
Ellen Louise Axson Wilson Edith Bolling Wilson	1913–1921
Florence Kling Harding	1921–1923
Grace Goodhue Coolidge	1923–1929
Lou Henry Hoover	1929–1932
Eleanor Roosevelt Roosevelt	1932–1945
Bess Wallace Truman	1945–

Suggested Groupings for Models
IN
"PAGEANT OF THE MISTRESSES OF THE WHITE HOUSE"

1. Martha Washington

2. Abigail Adams
   Martha Jefferson Randolph
   Dolly Madison
   Elizabeth Monroe
   Louisa Johnson Adams

3. Emily Donelson
   Sarah Angelica Van Buren
   Mrs. William Harrison (mention only)
   Lucretia Christian Tyler and
   Julia Gardiner Tyler
   Sarah Childress Polk

4. Betty Taylor Dandridge (Zachary Taylor)
   Abigail Fillmore
   Jane Pierce
   Harriet Lane Johnston (James Buchanan)

5. Mary Todd Lincoln

6. Martha Johnson Patterson (Johnson)
   Julia Dent Grant
   Lucy Webb Hayes

"Pageant of the Mistresses of the White House"

    Lucretia Garfield
    Mary Arthur McElroy (Chester Arthur)

7. Frances Folsom Cleveland

8. Caroline Scott Harrison } (Benjamin Harrison)
    Mary Harrison McKee
    Ida Sexton McKinley

9. Edith Carow Roosevelt
    Helen Herron Taft

10. Ellen Axson Wilson } (Woodrow Wilson)
     Edith Bolling Wilson
     Florence Kling Harding

11. Grace Goodhue Coolidge
     Lou Henry Hoover
     Eleanor Roosevelt
     Bess Truman

Colonial stage setting for first four groups.
Civil War stage setting for groups 5 and 6.
Late Victorian setting for groups 7 and 8.
More recent setting for groups 9, 10 and 11.

It has been suggested that it would be desirable at this point to suggest ways in which the costumes might be obtained for the presentation of this Pageant. In communities of any size there are often long established families who have heirloom gowns which have been handed down in the family for several generations, which is one possible source. In many communities over the nation there are members of families of past presidents who often have cherished garments worn by their relatives when in the White House. If it is not possible to borrow these dresses it is altogether likely that anyone handy with a needle could copy them, not necessarily in expensive material, but this could be done in cheaper material such as paper cambric, which in the evening would pass muster very nicely. If authentic costumes can not be obtained, from the illustrations in this book satisfactory copies could be made. Civic and little theaters often have wardrobes of old costumes, which those who present this Pageant might either borrow or rent. Costume houses are another source of help. In schools and colleges, which have courses in sewing, it would be a very interesting and valuable project for such departments to make the costumes. Even paper might be used. The ingenuity, the skill and the deeper interest aroused in the young students by assisting in the costuming would be of real value to them.

Suggested Quiz for History Students

AT HOME OR IN SCHOOL

Question 1. Give a list of all Presidents of the United States with dates of their administrations.

Question 2. How many Presidents have had two terms?

Question 3. From what states have our Presidents come? List Presidents by States.

Question 4. Which state has provided the greatest number of Presidents?

Question 5. What were the outstanding events during each one's term? Answer in not more than 200 words for this question.

Question 6. What towns, counties, or other places in your state were named for Presidents?

Question 7. To what President is your state especially indebted (up to and including Herbert Hoover), and why? Answer in not more than 100 words.

Question 8. Did any Presidents come from your state (either by birth or long residence)? If so, what ones? And for what were they especially distinguished? Answer in not more than 200 words.

Question 9. What three Presidents (up to and including Herbert Hoover) do you consider made the greatest contribution to the welfare of the country, and why? Answer in not more than 100 words.

At Home or in School

Question 10. If you are a boy, what President would you have preferred to have been (up to and including Herbert Hoover), and why? Answer in not more than 100 words.

Question 11. If you are a girl, what First Lady would you have preferred to have been (up to and including Mrs. Herbert Hoover)? Answer in not more than 100 words.

Question 12. To what three White House families would you have preferred to belong? Answer in not more than 100 words.

The first eight questions are purely factual so books and other authorities can be consulted. Answers to the last four questions are to be based on your own opinion after consulting various authorities.

Only those who are not living or who are completely out of politics have been included in this Quiz. For the Pageant is wholly non-partisan and non-political in its spirit.